# VEGETARIAN COOKERY

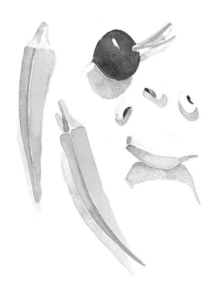

# VEGETARIAN COOKERY

## ROSE ELLIOT

## NOTE

1. All recipes serve four unless otherwise stated.

2. All spoon measurements are level. Spoon measures can be bought in both imperial and metric sizes to give accurate measurement of small quantities.

3. All eggs are sizes 2 or 3 unless otherwise stated.

4. All sugar is granulated unless otherwise stated.

5. Preparation times given are an average calculated during recipe tasting.

6. Metric and imperial measurements have been calculated separately. Use one set of measurements only as they are not exact equivalents.

7. Cooking times may vary slightly depending on the individual oven. Dishes should be placed in the centre of an oven unless otherwise specified.

8. Always preheat the oven or grill to the specified temperature.

9. If using a fan-assisted oven, follow the manufacturer's instructions for guidance on temperature adjustments.

10. Recipes marked **V** are suitable for vegans.

The text in this book has been adapted from *The New Vegetarian Cookbook*, originally published by Octopus Books Limited in 1986

This edition published in 1988 by the Octopus Publishing Group Plc, Michelin House, 81 Fulham Road, London SW3 6RB

ISBN 0 86273 475 4

Typeset by J&L Composition Ltd, Filey, North Yorkshire
Printed in Italy

# CONTENTS

# BREAKFASTS

**B**reakfast can be an enjoyable meal, especially a vegetarian one! In fact if you think about it, you'll probably find that you often eat a vegetarian-style breakfast anyway. So if you want to change over to the vegetarian way of eating, this can be a good meal to start with. There is plenty to choose from, and you may find that 'going vegetarian' at breakfast actually means you eat in a more varied and interesting way than before.

*Fruit Feast (recipe, page 8)*

# FRUIT FEAST

*3 ripe peaches, stones removed and flesh sliced*
*3 sweet apples, cored and diced*
*225 g (8 oz) black or green grapes, halved and seeded*
*225 g (8 oz) strawberries, hulled and halved or quartered*
*150 ml (¼ pint) orange juice*

Topping:
*225 g (8 oz) low-fat soft white cheese*
*150 ml (¼ pint) milk*
*1 teaspoon clear honey*

To decorate:
*50 g (2 oz) flaked almonds, toasted*

**Preparation time:** 30 minutes

1. Put all the fruit into a large bowl, add the orange juice and mix gently. Spoon this mixture on to a large flat serving dish.
2. Put the soft white cheese into a bowl and mix with a fork until creamy, then gradually blend in the milk and honey to make a thick, smooth consistency.
3. Spoon this over so that some of the fruits show prettily round the edges, then sprinkle the almonds on top. Serve with warm Wheatgerm, honey and raisin muffins (page 13).

# BREAKFAST PANCAKES

*100 g (4 oz) plain wholewheat flour*
*½ teaspoon salt*
*2 eggs*
*300 ml (½ pint) skimmed milk*
*2 tablespoons melted butter or margarine*
*extra butter for frying*

**Preparation time:** 2–3 minutes
**Cooking time:** about 3–4 minutes for each pancake

1. Put all the ingredients into a food processor or blender and blend until smooth; or put the flour and salt into a bowl, mix in the eggs, then gradually beat in the milk and melted fat.
2. Heat 10 g (¼ oz) butter in a small frying pan and, when it sizzles, pour off the excess, so that the pan is lightly greased.
3. Keep the frying pan over a high heat, then pour in 2 tablespoons of batter, and tip the frying pan so that the batter runs all over the base.
4. Cook the pancake until it is set on top and golden brown underneath, then flip the pancake over and cook the other side. Serve at once.

# BANANA MUESLI

*100 g (4 oz) rolled oats*
*50 g (2 oz) sunflower seeds*
*300 ml (½ pint) water*
*2 tablespoons clear honey*
*2 large bananas, peeled and sliced*
*225 g (8 oz) black grapes, halved and seeded*
*grated rind of 1 large well-scrubbed orange and 1 large well-scrubbed lemon*
*50 g (2 oz) flaked almonds, toasted*

**Preparation time:** 2 minutes, plus soaking

Ⅴ Suitable for vegans
The oats give this muesli a natural creaminess, and this is increased if you can leave them to soak overnight in the water. If you also soak the sunflower seeds, they will begin to germinate, adding extra health-giving enzymes to put a spring into your step!

1. Put the rolled oats and sunflower seeds into a bowl with the water; leave to soak overnight if possible.
2. Mix well until creamy, then add the honey, bananas, grapes and orange and lemon rind.
3. Spoon into four small dishes and sprinkle with toasted flaked almonds.

*CLOCKWISE FROM THE TOP: Fruit feast, Breakfast pancakes; Banana muesli*

# HUNZA APRICOTS WITH THICK YOGURT

250 g (9 oz) Hunza apricots, washed
water, to cover

To serve:
225 g (8 oz) thick plain yogurt, Greek or
   home-made (see below)

**Preparation time:** 5 minutes, plus
soaking
**Cooking time:** 10 minutes

These are whole wild apricots which are
dried without preservatives and are there-
fore brown in colour instead of orange.
They have a wonderful flavour and a
natural sweetness – really delicious!

1. Put the apricots into a medium-sized
saucepan and cover generously with water.
Leave to soak for a couple of hours if
possible (or, even better, overnight).
2. Simmer the fruit over a gentle heat,
without a lid on the saucepan, until the
fruit is very tender and the liquid has
reduced to a syrup. Serve hot or cold, with
the yogurt.

# HOME-MADE YOGURT

600 ml (1 pint) fresh skimmed milk
4 tablespoons skimmed milk powder
1 tablespoon plain live yogurt

**Preparation time:** 2 minutes
**Cooking time:** 4 minutes, plus 5–8 hours
setting time

Yogurt is easy to make at home. Make sure
that the yogurt you use for the 'starter' is
really 'live': read the label carefully, or buy
it from your local healthfood shop.
1. Put the milk into a saucepan and bring
to the boil, then remove from the heat and
cool to tepid.
2. Put in the skimmed milk powder and
yogurt, and whisk to make sure it's all well
blended.
3. Scald a bowl or jar with boiling water to
sterilize and warm it, then pour in the

yogurt mixture. Cover the container with
a piece of foil, then wrap it in a towel, to
help keep the heat in.
4. Place the mixture in a warm (but not too
hot) place such as an airing cupboard or
corner by a radiator. Then leave the yogurt
undisturbed for 5–8 hours, until it has set.
If you then put it into the refrigerator, it
will firm up even more.
Save a tablespoon of this batch of yogurt to
start off your next one. You will find that
the next few batches will get thicker and
better each time, but after a while you may
get a batch that's a bit on the 'thin' side,
and then you'll need to buy a new carton to
start you off again.

# PORRIDGE

50 g (2 oz) rolled oats (or oats up to the
   150 ml (¼ pint) mark on a measuring jug)
300 ml (½ pint) water
pinch of salt

**Preparation time:** 2 minutes
**Cooking time:** about 2 minutes

**V** Suitable for vegans
A bowl of steaming hot porridge makes a
delicious, and very healthy, start to the
day, and its very simple to make!
1. Put the oats and water into a saucepan
with the salt. Stir over a moderate heat for
about 2 minutes, until thickened. If the
porridge is too thick, add more water.
Serve immediately.

*FROM THE TOP: Hunza apricots with thick yogurt;
Porridge*

# ORANGE AND GRAPEFRUIT REFRESHER WITH MINT SORBET

2 large grapefruits
2 large oranges
little clear honey
4 sprigs of mint, to decorate

Mint sorbet:
2 tablespoons clear honey
150 ml (5 fl oz) water
2 tablespoons finely chopped mint

**Preparation time:** 20 minutes, plus freezing

Ⅴ Suitable for vegans
1. First make the sorbet. Mix together the honey, water and mint, then pour into a shallow container and freeze until the mixture is half solid. Break up the mixture with a fork, then freeze until firm.
2. With a small, serrated knife, and holding the fruit over a bowl, cut all the skin and pith from the grapefruits and oranges. Cut the segments from between the pieces of skin. Sweeten with honey to taste, then divide the fruit between four bowls.
3. Put a spoonful of sorbet on each, decorate with mint and serve immediately.

# MANGO COMPOTE

4 large ripe mangoes, halved, skinned and
    stones removed
150 ml (¼ pint) water

**Preparation time:** 2 minutes

Ⅴ Suitable for vegans
Mangoes are a particularly good source of zinc and make a delicious breakfast treat.
1. Cut the mango flesh into large even-sized pieces, reserving a few slices for decoration. Put half a cupful of these into the food processor or blender goblet with the water and purée until very smooth.
2. Put the remaining mango into a glass serving dish. Add the puréed mango, which provides a thick sauce, stir well to coat evenly and top with the reserved mango slices. Serve chilled.

# WHEATGERM, HONEY AND RAISIN MUFFINS

MAKES 12
butter for greasing
100 g (4 oz) wheatgerm
2 teaspoons baking powder
pinch of salt
75 g (3 oz) raisins
4 tablespoons clear honey
50 g (2 oz) butter or margarine, melted
2 eggs
about 6 tablespoons milk

CLOCKWISE FROM THE TOP: Orange and grapefruit refresher with Mint sorbet; Mango compote; Wheatgerm, honey and raisin muffins

**Preparation time:** 15 minutes
**Cooking time:** 15–20 minutes
**Oven:** 180°C, 350°F, Gas Mark 4

These muffins contain the goodness of wheatgerm and raisins, and are quick and easy to make. They're delicious served warm from the oven with Fruit feast (page 8), or as a healthy snack.
1. Grease a bun or muffin tin with butter. Put the wheatgerm, baking powder, salt and raisins into a bowl, then add the honey, butter or margarine and eggs.
2. Mix until blended, then stir in enough milk to make a fairly soft mixture which drops heavily from the spoon when you shake it.
3. Put heaped tablespoons of the mixture into the bun tin, dividing the mixture between twelve sections. Bake in a pre-heated oven for 15–20 minutes, until the muffins have puffed up and feel firm to a light touch. Serve warm.

# BANANA-BERRY SHAKE

**SERVES 1**
*1 banana*
*100 g (4 oz) fresh or frozen strawberries, hulled*
*150 ml (¼ pint) water*
*2 teaspoons clear honey (optional)*

**Preparation time:** 4 minutes

**V** Suitable for vegans
Another drink which is filling enough to make a complete breakfast or lunch.
1. Cut the banana into chunks and place in a blender with the strawberries and water, reserving one strawberry for decoration. Process to a smooth cream, adding a little more water if required. Sweeten with honey, if liked, and decorate with the reserved strawberry.

# MANGO AND ORANGE REFRESHER

**SERVES 1**
*1 medium mango, halved, skinned and pitted*
*150 ml (¼ pint) freshly squeezed orange juice*

To decorate:
*slice of orange*
*sprig of mint*

**Preparation time:** 5 minutes

**V** Suitable for vegans
This makes a wonderful quick breakfast or pick-me-up for when you feel your energy level is flagging. Make sure that the mango is really ripe: it should yield to gentle pressure.
1. Cut the mango into even-sized chunks and place in a blender with the orange juice. Process to a smooth purée, adding a little cold water if it is too thick. Serve in a tall glass, decorated with the orange slice and sprig of mint.

# ALMOND MILK

**SERVES 1**
*50 g (2 oz) almonds*
*150 ml (¼ pint) cold water*
*slices of lime, to decorate*

**Preparation time:** 4 minutes
**Cooking time:** 3 minutes

**V** Suitable for vegans
This looks like dairy milk, but tastes far more delicate and delicious. It is filling and nutritious, and with fresh fruit makes a good breakfast or lunch.
1. Place the almonds in a small pan, cover with cold water and bring to the boil. Boil for 1 minute, then remove from the heat, drain and cover with cold water. Pop the almonds out of their skins with your fingers and place in a blender. Grind as finely as possible.
2. Gradually add cold water to make a smooth liquid. You can strain this liquid into a glass for a thin smooth drink, but it is equally nice with the ground almonds left in. Decorate with slices of fresh lime.

*FROM THE LEFT: Banana-berry shake; Mango and orange refresher; Almond milk*

# SIMPLE DISHES

When you begin to prepare vegetarian meals one of the main problems is deciding how to plan a balanced meal without meat. The easiest way is to decide on a vegetarian protein dish (containing eggs, cheese, pulses or nuts) and think of this as the 'meat' then plan around it in the usual way. There are many possibilities and you probably already have several favourite main vegetarian dishes like savoury quiches or pizzas.

*Quick Pizza (recipe, page 26)*

# EASY TOMATO SOUP

2 tablespoons olive oil
1 onion chopped
350 g (12 oz) potatoes, peeled and diced
450 g (1 lb) fresh tomatoes, peeled and sliced,
    and 1 x 400 g (14 oz) can tomatoes
900 ml (1½ pints) light vegetable stock
salt
freshly ground black pepper
fresh basil or parsley, to garnish (optional)

**Preparation time:** 20 minutes
**Cooking time:** about 40 minutes

ⱴ Suitable for vegans

1. Heat the oil in a large saucepan and add the onion. Fry for 5 minutes, then put in the potatoes and tomatoes and continue to cook over a low heat for 10 minutes, stirring occasionally.

2. Add the stock, season to taste with salt and pepper and bring to the boil. Cover and simmer for 15–20 minutes, until the potatoes are soft.
3. Blend the soup until smooth. Reheat gently. Serve in heated bowls with a garnish of fresh basil or parsley, if liked.

# LEEK AND POTATO SOUP

25 g (1 oz) vegetarian margarine
350 g (12 oz) trimmed leeks, washed and
    sliced
750 g (1½ lb) potatoes, peeled and diced
3 teaspoons vegetarian stock powder
salt
freshly ground black pepper
900 ml (1½ pints) water

**Preparation time:** 20 minutes
**Cooking time:** about 30 minutes

ⱴ Suitable for vegans

1. Melt the fat in a large saucepan, then add the leeks and potatoes and fry very gently, with a lid on the pan, for 10 minutes, stirring often.
2. Sprinkle the stock powder and a little

salt and pepper over the potatoes and leeks, stir, then continue to cook gently, still covered, for a further 10 minutes, stirring often. It doesn't matter if the vegetables brown slightly, but don't let them get too brown.
3. Add the water, stir, then simmer for 5–10 minutes, until the vegetables are cooked. Check the seasoning, then serve.

# VEGETABLE SOUP WITH NORI

2 tablespoons olive oil
2 onions, peeled and chopped
4 celery sticks, diced
225 g (8 oz) carrots, scraped and diced
350 g (12 oz) courgettes, trimmed and diced
225 g (8 oz) Chinese leaves or cabbage,
    shredded
4 garlic cloves, crushed
2 teaspoons vegetarian stock powder
900 ml (1½ pints) water
salt
freshly ground black pepper

To garnish:
2–4 sheets of nori, crisped over a gas flame or
    under a grill, then crumbled, (optional)

**Preparation time:** 30 minutes
**Cooking time:** about 25 minutes

ⱴ Suitable for vegans

This is a delicious soup which can be varied according to whatever vegetables are available. It is good made with leeks instead of the courgettes. I think the sprinkling of nori, which is a variety of seaweed, gives the soup a tangy, salty flavour and it's full of minerals and vitamins.

1. Heat the olive oil in a large saucepan and add the onions, celery and carrots. Fry gently for 5 minutes, without letting the vegetables brown, then add the courgettes, Chinese leaves or cabbage and garlic. Stir, and fry gently for a further 5 minutes.

2. Add the stock powder, cook for 2–3 minutes more, then stir in the water. Bring to the boil, then let the soup simmer for about 10 minutes, until the vegetables are just tender.
3. You can serve the soup as it is, but I think it's better if you liquidize two cupfuls, then stir these back into the soup. This has the effect of slightly thickening the soup.
4. Season to taste. Serve the soup in bowls, and sprinkle with the nori, if you're using this, or serve the nori separately in a small bowl for people to sprinkle over the top of their soup if they like.

*CLOCKWISE FROM THE TOP: Easy tomato soup; Vegetable soup with nori; Leek and potato soup*

# CHEESE DIP WITH CRUDITÉS

SERVES 2
150 g (5 oz) vegetarian Cheddar-type cheese
40 g (1½ oz) butter or margarine
6 tablespoons milk
3–4 drops Tabasco sauce
salt
freshly ground black pepper
4 celery sticks, cleaned and trimmed
4–6 carrots, scraped
8 radishes
1 small green pepper
1 small cauliflower
sprig of parsley, to garnish

**Preparation time:** 10 minutes

1. Grate the cheese, then beat the butter or margarine until soft. Gradually add the cheese and milk, beating until smooth; or blend these ingredients together in the food processor.
2. Add the Tabasco sauce and salt and pepper to taste.
3. Cut the celery sticks into 10 cm (4 inch) lengths, slice the carrots, halve the radishes if large, slice and seed the green pepper and divide the cauliflower into florets.

4. Spoon the cheese dip into a small serving dish. Garnish with a sprig of parsley. Arrange a selection of crudités neatly around the dip.

# HUMMUS

225 g (8 oz) dried chick peas, soaked and
    cooked (page 132–3) or 2 x 400 g (14 oz)
    cans chick peas
2 garlic cloves, crushed
4 teaspoons sesame cream (tahini)
2 tablespoons olive oil
2 tablespoons lemon juice
salt
freshly ground black pepper

To serve:
extra olive oil
paprika
slices of lemon
black olives (optional)

**Preparation time:** 5 minutes

Ⴘ Suitable for vegans
1. Drain the chick peas, reserving the liquid. Put them into a food processor or blender with 120 ml (4 fl oz) of the reserved liquid, the garlic, sesame cream, olive oil and lemon juice. Blend until smooth. Season to taste with salt and pepper, then spoon into a serving dish.
2. Pour a little olive oil over the top, then sprinkle with paprika and garnish with lemon slices and olives. Serve with warm pitta bread cut in half or into finger-length pieces.

# TSATSIKI

1 large cucumber, peeled and diced
salt
250 g (9 oz) thick Greek yogurt
4 tablespoons chopped mint
2 garlic cloves, crushed
freshly ground black pepper
mint leaves, to garnish

**Preparation time:** 10 minutes, plus draining

1. Put the cucumber into a sieve or colander and sprinkle with salt. Set a weight on top and leave for 30 minutes.
2. Rinse and pat dry on paper towels. Put into a bowl with the yogurt, mint, garlic and pepper. Stir well, and season.

3. Put into a shallow serving dish and garnish with mint leaves.

*CLOCKWISE FROM THE TOP: Cheese dip with crudités; Hummus; Tsatsiki*

# WHOLEWHEAT CHEESE AND ONION PIE

*225 g (8 oz) plain 85 or 100 per cent
    wholewheat flour*
*½ teaspoon salt*
*100 g (4 oz) butter or margarine*
*3 tablespoons cold water*

*Filling:*
*3 large onions, peeled and sliced*
*175 g (6 oz) grated Cheddar cheese*
*salt*
*freshly ground black pepper*
*freshly grated nutmeg*

**Preparation time:** 20 minutes
**Cooking time:** 35 minutes
**Oven:** 220°C, 425°F, Gas Mark 7

1. Cook the onions in 2.5 cm (1 inch) boiling salted water for 5 minutes, to soften slightly. Drain and cool.
2. Meanwhile, make the pastry. Sift the flour into a large bowl, adding the residue of bran from the sieve if you're using 100 per cent wholewheat flour. Add the salt, then rub in the butter with your fingertips until the mixture looks like fine breadcrumbs.
3. Mix to a dough with the water, then roll out half the pastry to fit a 20–23 cm (8–9 inch) pie plate.

4. Mix the cheese with the onions, season to taste with salt and pepper and sprinkle with nutmeg.
5. Spoon the mixture on top of the pastry. Roll out the remaining pastry to fit the top; trim and press the edges together. Bake in a preheated oven for 30 minutes.

*Variation:* For Onion and Soured Cream Pie, use 150 ml (¼ pint) of soured cream and 2 teaspoons wholegrain or Dijon mustard instead of the grated cheese. For Onion Pie with a Cheesy Crust, sprinkle the pastry with 1 tablespoon grated Parmesan cheese, and reduce the quantity of cheese in the pie to 50 g (2 oz).

# STIR-FRIED VEGETABLES WITH NUTBALLS

*2 tablespoons oil*
*1 onion, peeled and chopped*
*1 garlic clove, crushed*
*piece of fresh root ginger, about the size of a
    walnut, peeled and finely grated*
*900 g (2 lb) prepared vegetables, shredded:
    carrots, courgettes, leeks, (as available)*
*salt*
*freshly ground black pepper*
*soy sauce, to taste*
*sprig of fresh coriander, to garnish*

*Nutballs:*
*1 onion, peeled, chopped and fried*
*150 g (5 oz) cashew nuts, roughly ground*
*75 g (3 oz) raw cauliflower, grated*
*40 g (1½ oz) fresh wholewheat
    breadcrumbs*
*2 tablespoons chopped fresh parsley*
*1 teaspoon mixed dried herbs*
*2 eggs*
*salt*
*freshly ground black pepper*
*oil for frying*

**Preparation time:** 10 minutes
**Cooking time:** about 12 minutes

1. First prepare the nutballs: simply mix everything together and form into balls about the size of walnuts.
2. Heat the oil in a frying pan and gently fry the nutballs for 2–3 minutes.
3. Remove them with a slotted spoon when they're ready and keep them warm while you cook the stir-fried vegetables.
4. Heat the oil in a large saucepan or wok and fry the onion, garlic and ginger for 5 minutes, then put in the vegetables and stir-fry for 2–3 minutes.
5. Season to taste with salt, pepper and soy sauce and serve at once with the nutballs, and garnish with a sprig of coriander.

*FROM THE TOP: Wholewheat cheese and onion pie;
Stir-fried vegetables with nutballs*

# TAGLIATELLE VERDE WITH MUSHROOMS AND SOURED CREAM

225–350 g (8–12 oz) tagliatelle verde
sprig of flat-leafed parsley or watercress, to
    garnish

Sauce:
1 onion, peeled and chopped
40 g (1½ oz) butter or margarine
1 garlic clove, crushed
350 g (12 oz) button mushrooms, wiped and
    sliced
300 ml (½ pint) soured cream
salt
freshly ground black pepper
freshly grated nutmeg

**Preparation time:** 5 minutes
**Cooking time:** about 30 minutes

When you're pressed for time, there's nothing to beat pasta for an easy, but satisfying, meal. This is a beautifully quick pasta dish with a wonderful, creamy mushroom sauce, which can be cooked while the pasta is boiling.
1. First make the sauce: fry the onion gently in 25 g (1 oz) butter or margarine for about 10 minutes until softened.
2. Then add the garlic and mushrooms and cook quickly for 2–3 minutes.
3. Add the soured cream, season with salt, pepper and nutmeg, then remove the pan from the heat.

4. Half-fill a large saucepan with lightly salted water and bring to the boil, then add the tagliatelle. Stir once, then leave the tagliatelle to cook, uncovered, for 10–15 minutes, until a piece feels tender but not soggy when you bite it.
5. Drain immediately into a colander, then tip back into the still-hot saucepan, add the rest of the butter or margarine and some salt and pepper. Stir for 1 minute until the fat has melted.
6. Quickly reheat the sauce, then tip the tagliatelle into a hot serving dish.
7. Pour the sauce over the top and serve at once, garnished with flat-leafed parsley or watercress sprigs. A crisp green salad goes with this pasta dish.

# SPINACH GNOCCHI

750 g (1½ lb) fresh spinach, cooked, drained
    and chopped or 450 g (1 lb) packet frozen
    chopped spinach, thawed
225 g (8 oz) soft white cheese made from
    skimmed milk
175 g (6 oz) curd cheese
50 g (2 oz) grated Parmesan cheese
2 egg yolks
salt
freshly ground black pepper
freshly grated nutmeg
wheatgerm
fresh basil, to garnish

To serve:
little butter or margarine
grated Parmesan cheese

**Preparation time:** 10 minutes
**Cooking time:** about 12 minutes

1. Purée the spinach in a blender or food processor. Put the purée back into the saucepan and dry off over the heat for a minute or two. Remove from the heat.
2. Put the skimmed milk cheese, curd cheese, Parmesan cheese and egg yolks into a bowl and mix together, then add the puréed spinach. Season with salt, pepper and nutmeg.
3. With wet hands, roll heaped teaspoonfuls of the mixture in wheatgerm. Half-fill a large saucepan with lightly salted water and bring to the boil.
4. Drop 6 or 8 of the gnocchi into the water and let them simmer very gently for about 4–5 minutes. When cooked they will float to the surface. Make sure the water does not go beyond simmering point, and remove the gnocchi as soon as they are

ready, or they may fall apart.
5. Drain them well, then put them into a warmed serving dish, dot with a little butter or margarine and keep them warm in a low oven while you cook another batch. Sprinkle with grated Parmesan cheese, garnish with fresh basil and serve immediately.

*FROM THE TOP: Tagliatelle verde with mushrooms and soured cream; Spinach gnocchi*

# QUICK PIZZA

oil for greasing
225 g (8 oz) 85 or 100 per cent self-raising
    wholewheat flour
2 teaspoons baking powder
½ teaspoon salt
50 g (2 oz) butter or margarine
8–9 tablespoons water

Topping:
2 onions, peeled and chopped
2 tablespoons oil
1 x 225 g (8 oz) can peeled tomatoes
2 tablespoons tomato purée
1–2 teaspoons oregano or mixed dried herbs
salt
sugar
freshly ground black pepper
100 g (4 oz) button mushrooms, wiped, sliced
    and fried
8–10 black olives
1 small green pepper, seeded, chopped and
    fried
75 g (3 oz) Gouda cheese, grated

**Preparation time:** 20 minutes
**Cooking time:** about 25–30 minutes
**Oven:** 220°C, 425°F, Gas Mark 7

This recipe makes one 30 cm (12 inch) pizza or two 20 cm (8 inch) ones.
1. Brush a large baking tray or 30 cm (12 inch) round pizza plate with oil.
2. Sift the flour and baking powder into a bowl, tipping in the residue of bran which will be left in the sieve if you're using 100 per cent wholewheat flour.
3. Add the salt, rub the fat into the flour with your fingertips, then pour in the water and mix to a pliable dough.
4. Either divide the dough in half and roll out into two 20 cm (8 inch) circles, or make one large circle to fit the pizza plate. Put the dough on the baking tray or plate and prick all over. Bake in a preheated oven for 10 minutes.
5. Meanwhile prepare the topping. Fry the onions in the oil for 10 minutes, then remove from the heat and add the peeled tomatoes, tomato purée, herbs and salt, sugar and pepper to taste.
6. Spread this mixture on top of the pizza base, top with the mushrooms, olives and green pepper and sprinkle with grated cheese. Bake for 15–20 minutes.

# NUTBURGERS IN SOFT BAPS

SERVES 12
2 onions, peeled and chopped
2 celery sticks, finely diced
100 g (4 oz) vegetarian margarine
2 teaspoons mixed dried herbs
2 tablespoons plain wholewheat flour
300 ml (½ pint) water
2 teaspoons vegetarian stock powder
2 tablespoons soy sauce
2 teaspoons yeast extract
450 g (1 lb) mixed nuts, roughly ground
225 g (8 oz) soft wholewheat breadcrumbs
salt
freshly ground black pepper

To finish:
dried breadcrumbs, to coat
olive oil for shallow frying

**Preparation time:** 20 minutes
**Cooking time:** about 20 minutes

Ⓥ Suitable for vegans
Ideal for a barbecue or when you have a crowd to feed.
1. Fry the onions and celery in the vegetarian margarine for 10 minutes, browning them lightly.
2. Add the herbs, stir for 1 minute, then mix in the flour and cook for a further 1–2 minutes.
3. Pour in the water and stir until thickened. Add the stock powder, soy sauce, yeast extract, nuts, breadcrumbs and salt and pepper to taste.
4. Allow the mixture to cool, then form into 12 flat burgers about 1 cm (½ inch) thick, and coat with dried breadcrumbs.
5. Cook on a flat, oiled baking sheet or frying pan over the barbecue. Serve in soft burger baps, with chutney and pickles as required and a crisp salad.

*FROM THE TOP: Quick pizza; Nutburgers in soft baps*

# CHILLI VEGETARIAN-STYLE

*175 g (6 oz) dried red kidney beans or 2 x
    400 g (14 oz) cans red kidney beans*
*1 onion, peeled and chopped*
*1 green pepper, seeded and chopped*
*1 tablespoon olive oil*
*1 garlic clove, crushed*
*1 x 400 g (14 oz) can tomatoes*
*150 g (5 oz) cooked green lentils (page 132–3)*
*1 teaspoon mild paprika*
*½–1 teaspoon chilli powder*
*salt*
*sugar*
*freshly ground black pepper*

**Preparation time:** 10 minutes, plus
soaking
**Cooking time:** about 2 hours, or 25
minutes if using canned beans

Ⓥ Suitable for vegans
1. If using dried kidney beans, soak for 6–8
hours, then drain. Cover with fresh water,
boil hard for 10 minutes, then simmer
gently for 1¼–1½ hours, until tender.
2. Fry the onion and pepper in the oil in a
large saucepan for 10 minutes, then add
the garlic and tomatoes.

3. Drain the red kidney beans and the
lentils and add the beans and lentils to the
tomato mixture. Flavour with the paprika
and chilli powder, salt, sugar and pepper
to taste.
4. Simmer for 10–15 minutes, season and
serve with rice.

# WHEAT-FILLED PITTAS

*225 g (8 oz) wholewheat grains, covered with
    cold water and soaked for 6–8 hours or
    overnight*
*2 tablespoons red wine vinegar*
*2 tablespoons olive oil (optional)*
*1 medium onion, purple if possible, peeled and
    sliced*
*2 tablespoons chopped fresh parsley or
    chopped fresh coriander*
*2 tomatoes, skinned and chopped*
*salt*
*freshly ground black pepper*
*1 head radicchio or a small lettuce, separated
    into leaves*
*4 wholewheat pitta breads, warmed*
*watercress sprigs, flat-leafed parsley or salad
    cress, to garnish*

**Preparation time:** 15 minutes, plus
soaking
**Cooking time:** 1 hour 15 minutes

Ⓥ Suitable for vegans
These hearty, nutty sandwiches make a
delicious and substantial main course and
can be filled with your own choice of salad
ingredients. Try endive and sliced tomatoes, cucumber and salad cress, or thinly
sliced courgettes and watercress.

   If wholewheat pitta bread are unobtain-
able split and fill large wholewheat baps.
Cut them in half to serve.

1. Drain the wheat, then put it into a
saucepan and cover with fresh water.
Bring to the boil and simmer for 1¼ hours,
or 25 minutes in a pressure cooker. Drain
and cool.
2. Put the red wine vinegar into a bowl
with the olive oil if you're using this and
add the wheat, onion, parsley or coriander,
tomatoes and a little salt and pepper to
taste.
3. Spoon the mixture with the radicchio or
lettuce leaves into warm wholewheat pitta
breads. Garnish with watercress sprigs,
flat-leafed parsley or salad cress.

*FROM THE LEFT: Wheat-filled pittas; Chilli
vegetarian-style*

# SAVOURY BEANSPROUT, MUSHROOM AND PINEAPPLE CRUMBLE

2 tablespoons oil
225 g (8 oz) button mushrooms, wiped and
    sliced
350 g (12 oz) beansprouts, washed and
    drained
225 g (8 oz) pineapple rings in natural juice,
    drained and chopped
2 tablespoons soy sauce
freshly ground black pepper

Topping:
100 g (4 oz) wholewheat plain flour
50 g (2 oz) vegetarian margarine
1 garlic clove, crushed
50 g (2 oz) cashew nuts, chopped
salt

**Preparation time:** 20 minutes
**Cooking time:** about 30 minutes
**Oven:** 200°C, 400°F, Gas Mark 6

Ⅴ Suitable for vegans
1. Heat the oil in a large saucepan or wok, then add the mushrooms, beansprouts and pineapple and stir-fry for 1–2 minutes, to cook very lightly.
2. Remove from the heat and add the soy sauce and freshly ground black pepper. Transfer the mixture to a shallow oven-proof serving dish or 4 individual rame-kins or ovenproof soup bowls.
3. To make the crumble, put the flour into a bowl and rub in the margarine to make a crumbly consistency, then mix in the garlic. Spoon this crumble over the beansprout mixture, so that it covers the top completely.
4. Sprinkle the cashew nuts on top and bake in a preheated oven for 20–30 minutes, until crisp and golden brown. Serve at once, with a crunchy side-salad made from shredded Chinese leaves and watercress.

# RED BEAN STEW WITH MILLET PILAFF

225 g (8 oz) millet
600 ml (1 pint) water
½ teaspoon salt
2 tablespoons olive oil
2 large onions, peeled and chopped
4 carrots, scraped and sliced
1 red pepper, seeded and chopped
1 green pepper, seeded and chopped
225 g (8 oz) dried red kidney beans, soaked
    and cooked, or 2 x 400 g (14 oz) cans red
    kidney beans
400 g (14 oz) can peeled tomatoes
salt
freshly ground black pepper

To garnish:
chopped fresh parsley
sprigs of parsley or coriander

**Preparation time:** 30 minutes, plus soaking and cooking beans
**Cooking time:** about 35 minutes

Ⅴ Suitable for vegans
1. Put the millet into a dry saucepan and toast over a medium heat for about 5 minutes, stirring all the time. The grains will brown lightly and some will start to 'pop'.
2. Add the water and salt and bring to the boil. Put a lid on the saucepan, turn down the heat and leave to cook for 15–20 minutes, until the millet is fluffy and has absorbed all the water.
3. Meanwhile prepare the stew. Heat the oil in a large saucepan and fry the onions, carrots and peppers gently, with a lid on the saucepan, for 15–20 minutes, until tender. Stir from time to time.
4. Drain the beans, reserving the liquid. Add the beans and tomatoes to the vegetables and season to taste. Cook over a low heat for 5–10 minutes, until heated through, adding a little of the reserved liquid if necessary. Serve the millet with the stew, sprinkled with chopped parsley and garnished with sprigs of parsley or coriander.

*Small, round pale golden grains, millet is familiar to most people as budgerigar food, but it is also very good for you. It combines the highest level of iron and protein of all the grains and can be served with most dishes which are normally accompanied by rice. If you want to increase your iron intake, buy flaked millet and add some to your breakfast muesli.*

*FROM THE TOP: Savoury beansprout, mushroom and pineapple crumble; Red bean stew with millet pilaff*

# VEGETABLE GRATIN

750 g (1½ lb) parsnips, peeled and sliced
1 large onion, peeled and sliced
225 g (8 oz) carrots, scraped and sliced
225 g (8 oz) courgettes, sliced
175 g (6 oz) cauliflower florets
225 g (8 oz) vegetarian Cheddar-type cheese, grated
salt
freshly ground black pepper

**Preparation time:** 5 minutes
**Cooking time:** about 25 minutes
**Oven:** 200°C, 400°F, Gas Mark 6

1. Boil the parsnips and onion in 2.5 cm (1 inch) water for 5–7 minutes, until nearly tender.
2. In a separate saucepan boil or steam the carrots, courgettes and cauliflower for about 5 minutes, until nearly tender.

3. Grease a large shallow ovenproof dish.
4. Put half the onion mixture in a layer in the base, sprinkle with a third of the cheese, the carrots, courgettes and cauliflower. Sprinkle with another third of the cheese and season with a little salt and pepper. Cover with the remaining onion mixture and finally top with the remaining cheese. Bake in a preheated oven for about 15 minutes.

# COUSCOUS WITH SPICED VEGETABLE STEW

350 g (12 oz) couscous
½ teaspoon salt dissolved in 600 ml (1 pint) tepid water
2 tablespoons olive oil
2 tablespoons chopped fresh parsley

Spiced Vegetable Stew:
2 tablespoons olive oil
2 onions, peeled and chopped
450 g (1 lb) carrots, scraped and cut into even-sized slices
2 teaspoons each cinnamon, ground cumin and ground coriander
100 g (4 oz) raisins
225 g (8 oz) dried chick peas, soaked, cooked until tender (page 132–3) then drained, or 2 x 400 g (14 oz) cans chick peas, drained, or 450 g (1 lb) frozen broad beans, peas or sweetcorn
900 ml (1½ pints) water
4 tablespoons tomato purée
salt
freshly ground black pepper
lemon wedges, to garnish

**Preparation time:** 20 minutes, plus soaking
**Cooking time:** about 1 hour

**V** Suitable for vegans
Couscous is a pre-cooked grain, so it only needs to be soaked in water, as described in the recipe, then heated through. The easiest way to do this is to put the couscous into a steamer set above the pan of stew.
1. Place the couscous in a bowl. Add the salted water and set aside.
2. Heat the oil in a large saucepan or the saucepan part of the steamer. Add the onions and carrots and fry gently for 10 minutes.
3. Add the spices and cook for 2–3 minutes, stirring.
4. Put in the raisins and the chick peas or beans, peas or corn, the water and tomato purée. Bring to the boil, then turn the heat down so that the stew just simmers.
5. By this time the couscous will have absorbed the water. Put it into the top part of the steamer, a metal colander or sieve, breaking it up a little with your fingers as you do so. Place over the stew, cover and steam for 25–30 minutes.
6. Season to taste. Stir the olive oil and parsley into the couscous and serve with the stew. Garnish with lemon wedges.

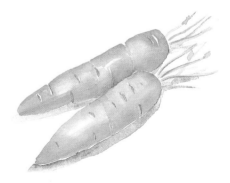

*FROM THE TOP: Vegetable gratin; Couscous with Spiced vegetable stew*

# SALAD STICKS

2 French sticks
vegetarian margarine
Dijon or wholegrain mustard or olive oil
1 lettuce, washed and shredded
450 g (1 lb) tomatoes, sliced
1 onion, peeled and sliced
1 cucumber, peeled and sliced
salt
freshly ground black pepper
spring onion curls or salad cress, to garnish

**Preparation time:** 25 minutes

**V** Suitable for vegans

1. Using a sharp knife, make a slit down the side of each French stick, ease it open without breaking it apart and scoop out a little of the loose crumb (this can be used for other recipes or made into crumbs and frozen).
2. Spread the inside of each French stick thinly with vegetarian margarine, mustard or olive oil, then pack each with the salad, filling them up well.

3. Press the slits together, wrap the loaves tightly in foil and chill until required. Garnish with spring onion curls or salad cress before serving.

# RATATOUILLE

2 large onions, peeled and chopped
450 g (1 lb) red peppers, cored, seeded and sliced
3 tablespoons olive oil
3 garlic cloves, crushed
450 g (1 lb) courgettes or marrow, cut into even-sized pieces
450 g (1 lb) aubergines, diced
750 g (1½ lb) tomatoes, skinned and chopped
salt
freshly ground black pepper
chopped fresh parsley, to garnish

**Preparation time:** 15 minutes
**Cooking time:** about 35 minutes

Serve this delicious, easy-to-make summer stew with plenty of crusty bread and a crisp salad on the side.
1. Fry the onions and peppers gently in the oil in a large pan without browning for 5 minutes.
2. Add the garlic, courgettes or marrow and aubergines. Stir, cover the saucepan and cook for 20–25 minutes, until all the vegetables are tender.
3. Stir in the tomatoes and cook, uncovered, for a further 4–5 minutes, to heat the tomatoes through. Season and sprinkle with chopped parsley.

FROM THE LEFT: Ratatouille; Salad sticks

# SPINACH LASAGNE

SERVES 6

2 large onions, peeled and chopped
1 tablespoon olive oil
2 garlic cloves, crushed
2 x 400 g (14 oz) cans tomatoes
salt
freshly ground black pepper
450 g (1 lb) packet frozen leaf spinach,
    thawed, or 900 g (2 lb) fresh spinach,
    cooked, drained and chopped
350 g (12 oz) cream cheese
100 g (4 oz) quick-cook lasagne

Topping:
soft wholewheat breadcrumbs
little butter or margarine

**Preparation time:** 30 minutes
**Cooking time:** about 30 – 40 minutes
**Oven:** 190°C, 375°F, Gas Mark 5

A big dish of lasagne makes a very welcoming meal and can be prepared well in advance. This version can be varied by the addition of more cheeses: 50 g (2 oz) grated Parmesan can be added to the spinach mixture, and 175–225 g (6–8 oz) Mozzarella can be sliced and layered with the lasagne, spinach mixture and sauce, for a richer (more fattening!) version. The whole dish (with or without the extra cheese) can be deep-frozen before cooking, if more convenient. Allow to thaw out completely before use, then cook as described in the recipe.

1. Fry the onions in the oil for 5 minutes, then add the garlic and fry for a further 5 minutes, without browning.
2. Purée 3 tablespoons of this onion mixture in a blender with the tomatoes and some salt and pepper to make a sauce. Add the rest of the onion to the spinach, together with the cream cheese and salt and pepper to taste.
3. Put a layer of spinach mixture into the bottom of a shallow, ovenproof dish and cover with a layer of lasagne, then half the tomato sauce. Repeat the layers, ending with the sauce. Sprinkle breadcrumbs all over the top of the lasagne and dot with butter or margarine.
4. Bake, uncovered, in a preheated oven for 20–30 minutes. Serve with a salad.

# SPICY LENTIL AND VEGETABLE STEW

1 large onion, peeled and chopped
2 tablespoons olive oil
225 g (8 oz) leeks, trimmed and sliced
225 g (8 oz) carrots, scraped and diced
2 garlic cloves, crushed
1 tablespoon white mustard seeds
1 tablespoon coriander seeds
1 teaspoon turmeric
small piece of fresh ginger, grated
225 g (8 oz) split red lentils
900 ml (1½ pints) water
1 tablespoon lemon juice
salt
freshly ground black pepper
fresh coriander leaves, if available, or
    fresh parsley, to garnish

**Preparation time:** 20 minutes
**Cooking time:** about 40 minutes

**V** Suitable for vegans
This is a delicious stew, spicy but not 'hot'. Serve it with mango chutney and a salad made from sliced tomatoes and onion rings.
1. Gently fry the onion in the oil for 5 minutes, then add the leeks and carrots, stir well and fry for a further 5 minutes. Add the garlic, mustard seeds, coriander seeds, turmeric, ginger and lentils and stir for 2–3 minutes.
2. Then pour in the water. Bring to the boil, then half cover the pan, reduce the heat and leave the mixture to simmer gently for 25–30 minutes, until the lentils are tender.
3. Add the lemon juice and season carefully to taste with salt and pepper. Serve garnished with fresh coriander or parsley leaves.

*FROM THE TOP: Spinach lasagne; Spicy lentil and vegetable stew*

# ALL-SEASON VEGETABLE CASSEROLE WITH WHOLEWHEAT DUMPLINGS

1 tablespoon olive oil
2 onions, peeled and chopped
2 celery sticks, sliced
225 g (8 oz) carrots, scraped and sliced
225 g (8 oz) parsnips, scraped and diced
2 garlic cloves, crushed
2 tablespoons 100 per cent self-raising
    wholewheat flour
600 ml (1 pint) water
2 teaspoons yeast extract
1 tablespoon vegetarian stock powder
3 tablespoons soy sauce
4 medium potatoes (about 200 g (7 oz) each),
    peeled and cut into chunks
75 g (3 oz) pearl barley
450 g (1 lb) button mushrooms, wiped and
    sliced
salt
freshly ground black pepper

Dumplings:
175 g (6 oz) 100 per cent plain wholewheat
    flour
1½ teaspoons baking powder
½ teaspoon salt
65 g (2½ oz) hard butter, grated
1 teaspoon yeast extract
water, to mix

**Preparation time:** 40 minutes
**Cooking time:** about 1 hour 10 minutes
**Oven:** 180°C, 350°F, Gas Mark 4

1. Heat the oil in a large saucepan, fry the onions, celery, carrots and parsnips for 10 minutes, stirring occasionally.
2. Stir in the garlic, flour, water, yeast extract, stock powder and soy sauce. Add the potatoes, barley and mushrooms.
3. Bring to the boil, then transfer to a large ovenproof dish, cover and bake in a preheated oven for 1 hour.

4. About half an hour before the casserole is ready, prepare the dumplings. Half-fill a large saucepan with water and bring to the boil.
5. Put the flour, baking powder, salt and butter into a medium bowl and mix well together. Then add the yeast extract and carefully pour in enough water to make a soft dough. Form the dough into eight even-sized balls.
6. Simmer the dumplings for about 20 minutes, until puffed up. Drain the dumplings and serve in the casserole.

# SHREDDED SPINACH WITH MUSHROOMS

1 tablespoon Dijon mustard
1 tablespoon wine vinegar
1 garlic clove, crushed
½ teaspoon salt
3 tablespoons olive oil
450 g (1 lb) tender spinach leaves, washed
    and finely shredded
100 g (4 oz) button mushrooms, wiped and
    sliced

**Preparation time:** 15 minutes

Ⅴ Suitable for vegans
1. Put the mustard, vinegar, garlic and salt into a bowl. Gradually stir in the oil to make a thick dressing, then add the spinach and mushrooms and stir gently, until all the ingredients are well coated.

*FROM THE TOP: All-season vegetable casserole with wholewheat dumplings; Shredded spinach with mushrooms*

# SPECIAL OCCASIONS

Newly-converted vegetarians often ask whether they should cook meat and fish for their family and friends. There is absolutely no need to do this because there are so many delicious vegetarian dishes to make that there's bound to be something to please even fussy eaters! In fact, I look upon entertaining as an excellent opportunity to show just how good vegetarian food can be.

*Stripy Vegetable Pâté with Sweet Pepper Sauce (recipe, page 47)*

## WATERCRESS AND STILTON SOUP

**SERVES 8**

*450 g (1 lb) leeks, trimmed, washed and sliced*
*2 bunches of watercress, washed*
*15 g (½ oz) butter or margarine*
*2 teaspoons vegetarian stock powder*
*900 ml (1½ pints) water*
*1 teaspoon cornflour*
*150 ml (¼ pint) single cream*
*75–100 g (3–4 oz) Stilton cheese, grated*
*salt*
*freshly ground black pepper*

**Preparation time:** 15 minutes
**Cooking time:** about 30 minutes

The combination of watercress and Stilton gives this soup a pleasant tang. The cheese can be coarsely grated and offered separately in a small bowl, if you prefer.
1. Fry the leeks and watercress in the butter or margarine in a large saucepan over a low heat for 15 minutes. Keep a lid on the saucepan, but stir the mixture from time to time, and don't allow it to brown.
2. Add the stock powder, cover and fry for a further 3–4 minutes. Pour in the water, bring to the boil, and simmer for about 10 minutes, stirring occasionally.

3. Blend the cornflour with the cream and add to the soup, together with the Stilton, then work in a blender until smooth. Season, reheat and serve.

*Variation:* soured cream and vegetarian Cheddar-type cheese can be used to replace the cream and Stilton. This gives a slightly more mellow flavour to the soup. Sprinkle a few chopped walnuts on top just before serving.

## CHILLED TWO-COLOUR MELON SOUP

**SERVES 8**

*1–2 Ogen melons, about 1½ kg (3 lb)*
*1–2 Charentais melons, about 1½ kg (3 lb)*
*2 tablespoons caster sugar (optional)*
*sprigs of fresh mint, to garnish*

**Preparation time:** 30 minutes

**V** Suitable for vegans
This soup is made from melons with contrasting flesh – orange and pale green. It's very easy to prepare and makes a stunning first course.
1. Halve the melons and remove the seeds. Then scoop out the flesh, keeping the two colours separate. Purée each batch in a blender and sweeten with the sugar, if preferred. Put the puréed melon into two separate jugs and chill.
2. To serve the soup, pour into bowls holding one jug at each side of the bowl, and pouring from both at the same time, so that each half of the bowl is a different colour as in the picture. Place a small sprig of mint in the centre of each bowl.

*A chilled two-coloured soup makes a very impressive starter for a summer dinner party. Instead of this pale green and orange melon soup, you could ring the changes by combining two other soups like a white leek and potato soup which would look – and taste – good with a green watercress soup or a bright pink Bortsch.*

*FROM THE LEFT: Watercress and stilton soup; Chilled two-colour melon soup*

# CARROT AND CORIANDER SOUP

SERVES 6

*15 g (½ oz) butter or margarine*
*450 g (1 lb) carrots, scraped and sliced*
*350 g (12 oz) leeks, washed and sliced*
*1 tablespoon coriander seeds, lightly crushed*
*pared rind of ½ lemon*
*2 teaspoons vegetarian stock powder*
*900 ml (1½ pints) water*
*1 tablespoon lemon juice*
*150 ml (¼ pint) single cream*
*salt*
*freshly ground black pepper*

**Preparation time:** 15 minutes
**Cooking time:** about 30 minutes

1. Melt the butter or margarine in a large saucepan, add the carrots and leeks and fry gently, covered, for 15 minutes, until the vegetables are almost soft.
2. Stir in the coriander, lemon rind and stock powder and fry for a further 2–3 minutes. Add the water, bring to the boil, and simmer for about 10 minutes. Add the lemon juice, cream and seasoning, then purée in a blender. Reheat and serve.

# MUSHROOM AND SHERRY PÂTÉ WITH MELBA TOAST

SERVES 6

*50 g (2 oz) butter or margarine*
*750 g (1½ lb) small firm button mushrooms, wiped and thinly sliced*
*3 tablespoons double cream*
*1 tablespoon dry sherry*
*salt*
*freshly ground black pepper*
*sprigs of parsley, to garnish*

Melba toast:
*6–8 slices wholewheat bread*

**Preparation time:** 15 minutes, plus chilling
**Cooking time:** 5–6 minutes

1. Heat the butter or margarine in a large saucepan and put in the mushrooms. Keeping the heat up high, fry the mushrooms quickly for 3–4 minutes, until just tender and lightly browned. If they begin to make liquid, the butter is not hot enough; the mushrooms should be dry.
2. Remove 18 perfect mushroom slices and reserve for the garnish. Work the rest in a blender with the cream, sherry and seasoning to taste.

3. Spoon the mixture into 6 individual ramekins or pâté dishes, level the tops, then press three of the reserved mushroom slices into the top of each, making a pattern with a sprig of parsley. Cool, then chill the pâtés.
4. To make the Melba toast, first toast the bread on both sides as usual, then, with a sharp knife, cut through the bread to split each piece in half, making each into two thin pieces.
5. Toast the uncooked sides until crisp and brown – the edges will curl up. Allow the toast to cool. Melba toast will keep for 2–3 days in an airtight tin.

*FROM THE LEFT: Mushroom and sherry pâté with melba toast; Carrot and coriander soup*

# STRIPY VEGETABLE PÂTÉ WITH SWEET PEPPER SAUCE

SERVES 6

*butter for greasing*

*225 g (8 oz) carrots, scraped and cut into even-sized pieces*

*225 g (8 oz) frozen or fresh broad beans, shelled*

*225 g (8 oz) frozen spinach, thawed*

*3 egg yolks*

*3 tablespoons double cream*

*salt*

*freshly ground black pepper*

*freshly grated nutmeg*

Sauce:

*1 red pepper, weighing about 175 g (6 oz)*

To garnish:

*sprigs of dill*

*twists of lemon or lime*

**Preparation time:** 40 minutes
**Cooking time:** 1½ hours
**Oven:** 160°C, 325°F, Gas Mark 3

This pâté is easy to make, yet looks most effective with its contrasting stripes.

1. Grease a 600 ml (1 pint) loaf tin with butter and line with a strip of greased greaseproof paper to cover the bottom of the tin and extend up the short sides.

2. Cook the carrots and broad beans in separate saucepans in only 1 cm (½ inch) boiling water until tender. Cook the spinach in a dry saucepan for 3–4 minutes.

3. Drain the vegetables thoroughly, saving the water (for the sauce), then blend separately, adding one of the egg yolks to each mixture. Add the cream to the puréed broad beans. Season the mixtures with salt and freshly ground black pepper, and add a little grated nutmeg to the spinach purée.

4. Spoon the spinach into the bottom of the prepared tin, levelling to make a smooth layer. Then carefully spoon the broad bean purée in an even layer on top, and finally add the carrot purée.

5. Cover with a piece of foil and bake in a preheated oven for 1 hour, removing the foil after 45 minutes. The pâté should be firm in the centre when touched lightly; leave it to cool in the tin. (The pâté can be completed to this stage the day before. When cold, cover with clingfilm and store in the refrigerator.)

6. To make the sauce, put the pepper under a hot grill until the skin is blackened and blistered all over. Then place in cold water and peel off the outer skin, which should come away easily. Remove the stalk and rinse away the seeds. Purée the pepper in a blender with 200 ml (7 fl oz) of the reserved cooking water. Season to taste

with salt and pepper, and chill until ready to serve.

7. When you serve the pâté, spoon a pool of sauce on to the centre of six small flat plates. Slip a knife round the sides of the pâté to loosen, it then turn it out of the tin and strip off the greaseproof paper. Cut the pâté into 2 cm (¾ inch) wide slices and place one on each plate on top of the sauce. Garnish with sprigs of dill and the lemon or lime twists before serving.

# BRIE FRITTERS WITH APRICOT CONSERVE

MAKES ABOUT 100
*900 g (2 lb) Brie*
*4 large eggs, beaten*
*wheatgerm, to coat*
*sunflower oil for deep-frying or olive oil for*
*    shallow-frying*
*apricot conserve, for serving*
*sprigs of parsley, to garnish*

**Preparation time:** 10 minutes, plus freezing
**Cooking time:** 20–30 minutes

1. Cut the cheese (including the skin) into bite-sized pieces. Dip each first into beaten egg, then into wheatgerm. The fritters need to be cooked from frozen, otherwise they fall apart, so open freeze for 1 hour.

2. Either deep-fry in sunflower oil or shallow-fry in hot olive oil, turning the fritters frequently to brown them all over.
3. Drain fritters well on paper towels and serve immediately with the apricot conserve.

# ASPARAGUS LOAF

SERVES 8
*1 small onion, peeled and grated*
*100 g (4 oz) grated Parmesan*
*100 g (4 oz) ground almonds*
*2 eggs*
*150 ml (¼ pint) single cream*
*salt*
*freshly ground black pepper*
*freshly grated nutmeg*
*450 g (1 lb) cooked, trimmed green asparagus*
*    (make sure that all the tough part has*
*    been removed)*

**Preparation time:** 40 minutes
**Cooking time:** 45–60 minutes
**Oven:** 190°C, 375°F, Gas Mark 5

It's well worth taking the time to arrange the asparagus neatly into the loaf tin. Season carefully as the Parmesan tends to be salty. This loaf makes a lovely summer dinner party dish, served with mayonnaise, mangetout peas and some crisp lettuce.
1. Grease a 450 g (1 lb) loaf tin and line with a long strip of greased greaseproof paper to cover the base and the short sides.
2. Mix together the onion, cheese, almonds, eggs and cream. Season the mixture with

salt, pepper and grated nutmeg.
3. Put a layer of this mixture in the bottom of the loaf tin, then arrange a layer of asparagus spears on top.
4. Continue in layers like this until all the ingredients are used up, ending with the nut mixture.
5. Bake in a preheated oven for 45–60 minutes, until risen and firm in the centre. Cool in the tin, then slip a knife round the sides and carefully turn out on to a plate. Strip off the paper.
6. Cut into slices, then cut in half again. Arrange the slices on a plate and serve with mangetout or a green salad.

*FROM THE TOP: Brie fritters with apricot conserve;*
*Asparagus loaf*

# INDIVIDUAL ASPARAGUS FLANS

MAKES 6

*350 g (12 oz) plain 85 per cent wholewheat*
*  flour*
*½ teaspoon salt*
*200 g (7 oz) butter or margarine*
*4–5 tablespoons cold water*

Filling:
*1 bunch asparagus, trimmed and cooked*
*300 ml (½ pint) single cream*
*2 egg yolks*
*salt*
*freshly ground black pepper*
*freshly grated nutmeg*

**Preparation time:** 30 minutes
**Cooking time:** about 35 minutes
**Oven:** 200°C, 400°F, Gas Mark 6;
    then: 180°C, 350°F, Gas Mark 4

1. Sift the flour and salt into a bowl, add
175 g (6 oz) of the butter or margarine,
then rub it into the flour with your
fingertips. Add the water and bind to a
dough.
2. Roll the dough out on a lightly floured
board, then use to line 6 x 10 cm (4 inch)
flan tins. Prick the flan bases and place in
the oven on a baking tray. Bake in a
preheated oven for 15–20 minutes, until
golden brown. Turn the oven down.

3. Trim the asparagus spears and divide
between the flans. Whisk the cream and
egg yolks together; season with salt,
pepper and nutmeg. Pour a little of this
mixture into each flan, on top of the
asparagus, dividing it equally between the
flans.
4. Return the flans to the oven and bake
for about 15 minutes, until the filling has
set. They should be just firm to the touch
and no more. Serve hot or cold with a crisp
salad.

# STUFFED BABY MUSHROOMS

SERVES 10

*50 open baby mushrooms, wiped*
*100 g (4 oz) Camembert cheese, diced*
*50 g (2 oz) butter*
*100 g (4 oz) walnut pieces, finely chopped*
*2 garlic cloves, crushed*
*2 tablespoons chopped fresh parsley*
*milk*
*sprigs of parsley, to garnish*

**Preparation time:** 20 minutes
**Cooking time:** about 15 minutes
**Oven:** 200°C, 400°F, Gas Mark 6

1. Remove the stalks from the mushrooms.
Chop the stalks and put into a bowl with
the Camembert (including the skin),
butter, nuts, garlic, parsley and a little
milk. Beat all the ingredients together
until well mixed but firm.
2. Place the mushrooms, stalk side up, in a
large shallow ovenproof dish or pizza dish.
Put a spoonful of the walnut mixture
on top of each mushroom, dividing it
between them.

3. Bake in a preheated oven for about 15
minutes. If the mushrooms produce some
liquid, strain this off before serving.

*Variation:* any soft cheese such as Brie or
Cambozola may be substituted for the
Camembert.

*FROM THE TOP: Individual asparagus flans;*
*Stuffed baby mushrooms*

# AVOCADO CREAM

*1 ripe avocado pear, halved, peeled and stone removed*
*1 tablespoon lemon juice*
*100 g (4 oz) curd or cream cheese*
*1 garlic clove, crushed*
*dash of red wine vinegar*
*few drops of Tabasco sauce*
*salt*
*freshly ground black pepper*
*mild paprika, to garnish*

**Preparation time:** 10 minutes

This is a delicious, pale green, creamy dip. It can also be used, by the way, as a wonderful dressing for a salad (instead of mayonnaise!) or as a first course, spooned on to crisp lettuce leaves, garnished with a sprinkling of paprika pepper and slices of lemon and tomatoes and served with hot Melba toast (page 45). Do make sure that the avocado is really ripe – it should 'give' easily when pressed at the stalk end, and feel generally soft (but not 'soggy' when cradled in your hand).

1. Mash the avocado pear flesh with the lemon juice, then gradually mix in the curd or cream cheese to make a smooth, creamy consistency.
2. Add the garlic, a few drops of wine vinegar, Tabasco sauce and season to taste with salt and pepper.
3. Spoon into a small bowl, smooth the top and sprinkle with some paprika. Guests can take a spoonful of this and eat it with the salad and other savouries.

# VEGETABLE KEBABS

SERVES 6
*36 small button mushrooms, wiped*
*1 aubergine (about 225 g (8 oz), cut into chunks about 2.5 cm (1 inch) long, 1 cm (½ inch) wide and 5 mm (¼ inch) thick, sprinkled with salt, left for 30 minutes, then rinsed and drained*
*1 medium red or green pepper, seeded and cut into strips about 2.5 cm (1 inch) long and 1 cm (½ inch) wide*
*24 baby pickling onions, peeled, or 2 onions, peeled and cut into chunks*
*6 small courgettes, total weight (about 350 g (12 oz), cut into slices 1 cm (½ inch) thick*

Marinade:
*3 tablespoons Dijon mustard*
*3 garlic cloves, crushed*
*3 tablespoons Barbados sugar*
*3 tablespoons soy sauce*
*3 tablespoons olive oil*
*1½ teaspoons salt*
*freshly ground black pepper*

*FROM THE TOP: Avocado cream; Vegetable kebabs*

**Preparation time:** 1 hour, plus draining and marinating
**Cooking time:** 10–15 minutes

Ⅴ Suitable for vegans
1. Thread the vegetables on to 12 skewers, putting on first a mushroom, then a piece of aubergine followed by a piece of red or green pepper, an onion and a chunk of courgette. Continue in this way until all the skewers are full.
2. Mix together all the ingredients for the marinade.
3. Lay the skewers flat on a non-metal tray, polythene container, large plate or casserole. Spoon the marinade over them, turning the skewers to make sure that all the vegetables are thoroughly coated with the mixture.
4. Leave to marinate for at least 1 hour, basting occasionally.
5. Cook the kebabs on the grid of the barbecue or under a preheated hot grill for 10–15 minutes, until the vegetables are tender. Serve the kebabs on a bed of brown rice with the remaining marinade in a small jug.

# BUTTERED BROCCOLI

**SERVES 8**
*1 kg (2 lb) broccoli, trimmed*
*50 g (2 oz) butter*
*salt*
*freshly ground black pepper*

**Preparation time** 10 minutes
**Cooking time:** 15–20 minutes

1. Place the broccoli in a steamer basket or metal colander over a pan of boiling water.
2. Cover and steam for 15–20 minutes until just cooked. Toss in the butter and season with salt and pepper.

# WILD MUSHROOM FEUILLETÉ

**SERVES 6**
Pastry:
*175 g (6 oz) fine ground wholewheat flour*
*½ teaspoon salt*
*100 g (4 oz) hard butter or block margarine*
*1 teaspoon lemon juice*
*about 6 tablespoons water*

Filling:
*15 g (½ oz) butter or margarine*
*450 g (1 lb) white button mushrooms, wiped and sliced*
*350 g (12 oz) oyster mushrooms (pleurotes), wiped and sliced*
*300 ml (½ pint) carton soured cream*
*300 ml (½ pint) carton single cream*
*1 garlic clove, crushed*
*salt*
*freshly ground black pepper*

To serve:
*350 g (12 oz) baby new potatoes, scraped*
*350 g (12 oz) carrots, scraped and cut into matchsticks*
*350 g (12 oz) broccoli*
*225 g (8 oz) mangetout, topped and tailed*
*lemon twists, to garnish*

**Preparation time:** 30 minutes, plus chilling
**Cooking time:** about 30 minutes
**Oven:** 230°C, 450°F, Gas Mark 8

Wild oyster mushrooms give a touch of luxury, and a delicious flavour and texture to this dish, but if you can't obtain them, simply use cultivated mushrooms.
1. Make the pastry according to the directions on page 61.
2. Roll the pastry out to a depth of about 3 mm (⅛ inch) and cut out 6 x 7.5 cm (3 inch) circles and 6 x 5 cm (2 inch) ones.
3. Put the circles on a baking tray and bake in a preheated oven for 10–12 minutes, until puffed up and golden brown.
4. Meanwhile, melt the butter or margarine and fry the button mushrooms and oyster mushrooms for 5 minutes, until tender.
5. Remove the mushrooms with a slotted spoon and boil the remaining liquid rapidly until reduced to 1 tablespoon. Add the mushrooms, soured cream, single cream, garlic and season to taste with salt and pepper.
6. Cook the vegetables separately until just tender – the potatoes will go in the bottom of a steamer saucepan with the carrots and broccoli on top. The mangetout should be cooked separately for about 3 minutes in a little boiling water. Drain the vegetables well.

7. To serve, reheat the mushroom mixture by stirring over a gentle heat. Place a large pastry circle on a warmed plate, with a serving of the mushroom mixture and liquid on top. Cover with one of the smaller pastry circles.
8. Arrange the vegetables in piles round the pastry. Garnish with a twist of lemon. Repeat with the remaining plates and serve at once.

*FROM THE TOP: Buttered broccoli; Wild mushroom feuillété*

# PANCAKES WITH RED PEPPER AND TOMATO FILLING

**SERVES 6**

Pancakes:

*100 g (4 oz) 85 or 100 per cent wholewheat*
  *flour*
*½ teaspoon salt*
*1 large egg*
*1 egg yolk*
*150 ml (¼ pint) milk*
*150 ml (¼ pint) water*
*2 tablespoons melted butter or oil*
*extra butter or oil for frying*

Filling:

*750 g (1½ lb) sweet red peppers*
*2 tablespoons olive oil*
*1 onion, peeled and chopped*
*1.5 kg (3 lb) tomatoes, skinned, seeded and*
  *chopped*
*salt*
*freshly ground black pepper*

To finish:

*300 ml (½ pint) soured cream or thick Greek*
  *yogurt*
*paprika*
*sprigs of parsley*

**Preparation time:** 30 minutes
**Cooking time:** about 1 hour 20 minutes
**Oven:** 190°C, 375°F, Gas Mark 5

Stuffed pancakes are a versatile and popular vegetarian dish. They're also a very practical one, because both the pancakes and the filling can be made in advance and deep-frozen. To freeze the pancakes, simply stack them up on top of each other with a layer of greaseproof paper between each one. Allow to cool, then pack in a polythene bag. Different fillings can be used instead of the red pepper mixture. One favourite that's beautifully easy to do is simply sliced ripe avocado tossed in a little lemon juice. Spoon a little avocado on each pancake and roll up as directed. Bake the pancakes for about 10–15 minutes, until heated right through.

1. First make the filling. Heat the red peppers under a hot grill until they're browned all over, and the outer skins will come off easily. Put the peppers into cold water and peel off the skins. Remove the stalk ends and seeds and cut into small pieces.

2. Heat the oil in a large saucepan and fry the onion for 10 minutes, then put in the peppers and tomatoes and cook, uncovered, for about 30 minutes, until the mixture is fairly thick and dry. Stir frequently towards the end of the cooking time to prevent burning. Season to taste with salt and pepper.

3. To make the pancakes, put all the ingredients into a food processor or blender and work until smooth. Alternatively, put the flour and salt into a bowl, mix in the eggs, then gradually add the milk, water and butter or oil to make a smooth, fairly thin batter.

4. Heat 10 g (¼ oz) butter or a little oil in a small frying pan; when it sizzles, pour off excess butter or oil, so that the frying pan is just glistening.

5. Keeping the frying pan over a high heat, give the pancake batter a quick stir, then put 2 tablespoonfuls into the pan. Tip it to make the batter run all over the bottom.

6. Cook the pancake for about 30 seconds, until the top is set and the underside is tinged golden brown. Flip the pancake over and cook the other side.

7. Remove the pancake with a palette knife and put it on to a plate. Make eleven more pancakes in the same way, piling them up on top of each other.

8. To assemble the dish, put a spoonful of the pepper and tomato mixture on each pancake and roll up neatly. Place the pancakes side by side in a shallow oven-proof dish. Give the cream a quick stir, then spoon this over the top of the pancakes. Sprinkle with paprika and cover with foil.

9. To finish the dish, bake the pancakes in a preheated oven for about 20 minutes, until heated through. Garnish with sprigs of parsley and serve at once.

# CHESTNUT, WALNUT AND RED WINE LOAF

**SERVES 8**

*1 onion, peeled and chopped*
*1 celery stick, finely chopped*
*25 g (1 oz) butter or margarine*
*4 garlic cloves, crushed*
*350 g (12 oz) cooked fresh or canned*
*chestnuts, roughly mashed*
*350 g (12 oz) cashew nuts, roughly ground*
*100 g (4 oz) walnuts, roughly ground*
*100 g (4 oz) Cheddar cheese, grated*
*150 ml (¼ pint) dry red wine*
*3 tablespoons chopped fresh parsley*
*1 tablespoon brandy*
*½ teaspoon paprika*
*½ teaspoon dried thyme.*
*2 eggs*
*salt*
*freshly ground black pepper*

To garnish:
*sprigs of parsley*
*tomato wedges*
*lemon slices*

**Preparation time:** 30 minutes
**Cooking time:** about 1½ hours
**Oven:** 190°C, 375°F, Gas Mark 5

1. Grease and line a 1 kg (2 lb) loaf tin with a long strip of greased greaseproof or non-stick paper to cover the base and the short sides of the tin.
2. Fry the onion and celery in the butter or margarine for 7 minutes, then add the garlic and cook for a further 2–3 minutes. Remove from the heat and add the remaining ingredients, seasoning well with salt and pepper.
3. Spoon the mixture into the prepared tin. Cover with a piece of foil and bake in a preheated oven for 1 hour, then remove the foil and continue cooking for a further 15 minutes, until firm in the centre.
4. Remove the loaf from the oven and allow to stand for 4–5 minutes, then loosen the edges by slipping a knife between the loaf and the tin.

5. Turn the loaf out on to a warmed serving dish. Garnish with parsley sprigs, tomato wedges and lemon slices.

# GARLIC MUSHROOMS WITH FRENCH BREAD

**SERVES 6**

*100 g (4 oz) butter*
*4 garlic cloves, crushed*
*750 g (1½ lb) button mushrooms, wiped and*
*quartered*
*salt*
*freshly ground black pepper*
*sprigs of parsley, to garnish*
*1 French stick, warmed, to serve*

**Preparation time:** 20 minutes
**Cooking time:** 2–3 minutes

This is a first course which can be ready in moments.
1. Melt the butter in a large saucepan and add the garlic.
2. When the butter is really hot (but not brown), put in the mushrooms. Fry these quickly for 2–3 minutes, so that they become tender but slightly crisp on the outside.
3. Divide the mushrooms between six hot, deep dishes (soup bowls are ideal), pour the butter over, and serve at once, with the warm French bread.

*FROM THE TOP: Chestnut, walnut and red wine loaf; Garlic mushrooms with French bread*

# FLAKY MUSHROOM ROLL

SERVES 6

*15 g (½ oz) butter or margarine*
*1 onion, peeled and chopped*
*225 g (8 oz) mushrooms, wiped and chopped*
*2 tablespoons chopped fresh parsley*
*100 g (4 oz) brown rice, cooked*
*salt*
*freshly ground black pepper*
*little raw egg yolk*
*sprigs of parsley, to garnish*

Rough-puff pastry:
*225 g (8 oz) fine ground wholemeal flour*
*1 teaspoon salt*
*175 g (6 oz) hard butter or block margarine,*
*    from the refrigerator*
*2 teaspoons lemon juice*
*about 8 tablespoons cold water*

**Preparation time:** 40 minutes, plus chilling
**Cooking time:** 30 minutes
**Oven:** 220°C, 425°F, Gas Mark 7

1. First make the pastry. Mix the flour and salt in a large bowl and grate in the butter. Add the lemon juice and water, then mix quickly to a fairly soft dough. Gather this into a ball, wrap in clingfilm and chill for at least 1 hour.
2. Roll the dough into an oblong. Mark this lightly into 3 equal sections, then fold the bottom third up and the top third down, to make 3 layers.
3. Seal the edges by pressing them lightly with your rolling pin (to trap the air), then give the pastry a quarter turn.
4. Repeat the rolling, folding and turning four times.

5. Heat the butter or margarine in a large saucepan and fry the onion and mushrooms quickly over a high heat for 2–3 minutes. Remove from the heat, add the parsley, rice, salt and pepper and leave to cool.
6. Divide the pastry in half, then roll each piece into a rectangle 30 x 25 cm (12 x 10 inches).
7. Place one of these rectangles on a baking sheet, carefully spoon the mushroom mixture on top, and brush the edges with cold water.
8. Put the second piece of pastry on top and press the edges together; trim. Make a few holes for the steam to escape, and brush with egg yolk.
9. Bake in a preheated oven for 30 minutes. Serve garnished with sprigs of parsley.

# RAINBOW FLOWER SALAD

SERVES 2

*4 leaves of curly endive, broken into even-*
*    sized pieces*
*1 small head of radicchio, broken into even-*
*    sized pieces*
*2 medium-sized cooked beetroots, cut into*
*    bite-sized chunks*
*6 spring onions, trimmed*
*8 radish roses (see right)*
*4 cherry tomatoes (if available), skinned*
*1 large carrot, scraped and chopped*
*10 cm (4 inch) piece of daikon (mooli or white*
*    radish), scraped and cut into several*
*    chrysanthemums (see right)*

**Preparation time:** 45 minutes

V Suitable for vegans
1. Arrange all the ingredients attractively on one or two large plates.

*To make daikon chrysanthemums, take a walnut-sized piece of daikon and make criss-cross cuts as close together as you can, without cutting through to the base. Sprinkle with salt, easing it gently between the cuts. Leave for 30 minutes, then rinse and carefully open the slits.*

*    Radish roses are made by cutting a row of petal shapes around a radish using a sharp knife, keeping them joined at the base. Cut more rows of petal shapes in between and above the first row and continue cutting until you reach the top of the radish. Place in iced water for several hours to open out.*

*FROM THE TOP: Flaky mushroom roll; Rainbow flower salad*

# CHEESE FONDUE

**SERVES 2**

*1 garlic clove, halved*
*175 ml (6 fl oz) dry white wine*
*450 g (1 lb) Emmenthal cheese, thinly*
*    sliced*
*2 teaspoons cornflour*
*2 tablespoons Kirsch or gin*
*few drops of lemon juice*
*freshly ground black pepper*
*freshly grated nutmeg*

*To serve:*
*1 French stick, cut into bite-sized pieces and*
*    warmed in the oven, or 1 crusty wholemeal*
*    loaf, cut into similar sized pieces and*
*    warmed in the oven*

**Preparation time:** 10 minutes
**Cooking time:** 20 minutes

1. Rub the garlic clove around the inside of a small saucepan, then discard. Put the wine into the pan and bring nearly to the boil. Add the cheese, stirring over a low heat until it has melted.
2. Blend the cornflour with the Kirsch or gin to form a smooth paste. Add to the wine and melted cheese, still stirring, until the mixture has thickened slightly.
3. Remove from the heat, add a few drops of lemon juice and season with pepper and nutmeg. Set the pan over a candle burner or fondue burner and serve immediately with the bread.

4. To eat, spear pieces of bread with long forks (or fondue forks, if you have them) then dip the bread into the fondue and eat it. Serve with Rainbow flower salad (page 61), which makes a refreshing contrast to the rich fondue, and the chunky pieces of vegetable can be used for dipping, too.

# VEGETABLES À LA GRECQUE

**SERVES 6**

*2 tablespoons olive oil*
*1 large onion, peeled and chopped*
*3 garlic cloves, crushed*
*1 medium cauliflower, trimmed, washed and*
*    broken into florets*
*350 g (12 oz) French beans, trimmed and cut*
*    into 2.5 cm (1 inch) pieces*
*175 g (6 oz) button mushrooms, wiped and*
*    cut into even-sized pieces*
*1 tablespoon coriander seeds, crushed*
*6 teaspoons lemon juice*
*2 teaspoons salt*
*freshly ground black pepper*

*To garnish:*
*chopped fresh parsley*
*few black olives*
*lemon twists*
*strips of red pepper*

**Preparation time:** 15 minutes, plus chilling
**Cooking time:** about 15–18 minutes

Ⅴ Suitable for vegans
This delicious, lightly spiced mixture can be made with other vegetables in season. Try replacing the cauliflower with baby Brussels sprouts, quartered, and the French beans with sliced leeks. Carrots would also make a colourful addition.

Vegetables prepared in this way can also be served as a light midday meal or as a supper dish with some grated cheese sprinkled on top.
1. Heat the oil in a large saucepan, then fry the onion for 5 minutes, without letting it brown.
2. Add the garlic and cauliflower and stir-fry for a further 5–6 minutes, then put in the beans, mushrooms and coriander seeds and continue to fry for about 2 minutes, until the mushrooms are beginning to soften.

3. Remove from the heat, add the lemon juice, salt and black pepper. Cool, then chill.
4. Serve on individual plates, sprinkled with chopped parsley and garnished with black olives, lemon twists and strips of red pepper.

*FROM THE TOP: Cheese fondue; Vegetables à la Grecque*

# SPINACH ROULADE WITH MUSHROOM AND SOURED CREAM FILLING

*900 g (2 lb) fresh spinach or 450 g (1 lb)*
  *chopped frozen spinach*
*15 g (½ oz) butter or margarine*
*salt*
*freshly ground black pepper*
*4 eggs, separated*
*little grated Parmesan cheese*
*celery leaves, to garnish*

Filling:
*15 g (½ oz) butter or margarine*
*175 g (6 oz) button mushrooms, wiped and*
  *sliced*
*300 ml (½ pint) soured cream*
*freshly grated nutmeg*

**Preparation time:** 15 minutes
**Cooking time:** about 30 minutes
**Oven:** 200°C, 400°F, Gas Mark 6

Like a savoury Swiss roll, this looks impressive and is always popular.
1. Cook the fresh spinach in a saucepan without water for about 10 minutes, until it is tender, then drain thoroughly and chop. Cook frozen spinach according to the instructions on the packet, then drain well. Add the butter or margarine, a little salt and pepper and the egg yolks.
2. Line a shallow 18 x 28 cm (7 x 11 inch) Swiss roll tin with greased greaseproof paper to cover the base of the tin and extend 5 cm (2 inches) up each side. Sprinkle with Parmesan cheese.
3. Whisk the egg whites until stiff but not dry and fold them into the spinach mixture. Pour the mixture into the prepared tin and bake in a preheated oven for 10–15 minutes, until risen and springy to touch.

4. While the roulade is cooking, make the filling. Heat the fat in a saucepan and fry the mushrooms quickly over a high heat (this keeps them dry) for 2–3 minutes. Then add the soured cream, a little salt, pepper and grated nutmeg and heat gently, just to warm through the cream. Don't let it boil.
5. Have ready a large piece of greaseproof paper dusted with Parmesan cheese and turn the roulade out on to this; strip off the first greaseproof paper.
6. Spread the filling over the roulade, then roll it up like a Swiss roll and slide it on to a warmed serving dish. Return to the oven for 5 minutes to heat through. Serve immediately, garnished with celery leaves.

# HOT STUFFED AVOCADOS

SERVES 8
*4 large ripe avocado pears*
*rind and juice of 1 well-scrubbed lemon*
*1 bunch of spring onions, trimmed and*
  *chopped*
*200 g (7 oz) skinned hazelnuts, chopped*
*175 g (6 oz) vegetarian Cheddar-type cheese,*
  *grated*
*4 tablespoons chopped fresh parsley*
*4 tablespoons dry sherry or wine*
*salt*
*freshly ground black pepper*
*lemon twists, to garnish*

**Preparation time:** 10 minutes
**Cooking time:** about 20 minutes
**Oven:** 200°C, 400°F, Gas Mark 6

1. Cut the avocado pears in half and remove the stones. Put the avocado halves, cavity side up, in a shallow casserole dish, then brush the cut surfaces with a little of the lemon juice.
2. Mix together the onions, hazelnuts, cheese, parsley and sherry or wine. Add the lemon juice, rind and season.
3. Divide this mixture between the avocado halves, and bake for 15–20 minutes. Garnish and serve immediately.

*FROM THE TOP: Spinach roulade with mushroom and soured cream filling; Hot stuffed avocados*

# SALADS

**A** crisp salad makes a delicious and refreshing meal. It is also very healthy because it contians enzymes and vitamins which are normally destroyed by cooking, and can be made from whatever mixture of fresh vegetables and fruits you have to hand. Salads need not be served just as summer meals; there's always some fruit or vegetable in season that can be used and winter salads can be delicious.

*Chicory, Orange and Watercress Salad (recipe, page 72)*

# DEEP-DISH SALAD BOWL

SERVES 2

4 lettuce leaves, shredded
100 g (4 oz) cold cooked potato, diced
4 tablespoons mayonnaise or soured cream, or
    a mixture of both
salt
freshly ground black pepper
100 g (4 oz) beansprouts, preferably home-
    grown
1 tablespoon olive oil
1 tablespoon wine vinegar
2 tomatoes, chopped
10 cm (4 inches) cucumber, cubed
2 tablespoons raisins
1 large carrot, finely grated
1 raw beetroot, peeled and finely grated
little salad cress or watercress, to garnish

**Preparation time:** 20 minutes

The joy of this salad is that the ingredients are arranged in layers in one large or two individual deep bowls and topped with a creamy dressing, so everything gets pleasantly mixed together as you plunge in your fork and eat the salad. This salad is quick to make if you save some cooked potato from a previous meal; this will keep in a covered bowl in the refrigerator for a day or two. Grated carrot and beetroot will also keep for 24 hours in the refrigerator (although there will be a small loss of vitamins). Other ingredients can be used in this salad: try it with shredded cabbage in place of the lettuce and diced celery instead of cucumber.

1. Put the shredded lettuce in the bottom of two deep dishes or soup bowls. Mix the potato with half the mayonnaise, soured cream or mayonnaise/soured cream mixture; season, then spoon into the bowls on top of the lettuce.

2. Mix the beansprouts with the oil, vinegar and some salt and pepper to taste. Put these on top of the potatoes, followed by the tomatoes, cucumber, raisins, grated carrot and beetroot, piling the mixture up attractively.

3. Spoon the remaining mayonnaise, soured cream or mayonnaise/soured cream mixture on top of the beetroot and sprinkle with some salad cress or watercress. Serve immediately.

# RED BEAN SALAD

SERVES 2

50 g (2 oz) frozen sweetcorn
100 g (4 oz) dried red kidney beans, cooked
    and drained (page 132–3), or 1 x 400 g
    (14 oz) can red kidney beans, drained and
    rinsed under the tap
1 large stick of celery, finely diced
1 large carrot, scraped and coarsely grated
1 spring onion, chopped, or 2 teaspoons finely
    chopped onion
1 tablespoon olive oil
1 tablespoon wine vinegar
salt
freshly ground black pepper

To serve:
4 crisp lettuce leaves
chopped fresh parsley

**Preparation time:** 15 minutes

V Suitable for vegans

1. Put the corn into a sieve and rinse under hot water to thaw, then place in a bowl with the red kidney beans, celery, grated carrot, chopped onion, oil, vinegar and seasoning. Mix well.

2. Arrange the lettuce leaves in two bowls, spoon the red kidney bean mixture on top and sprinkle with chopped parsley. If you're making this for 1 person, the remaining mixture will keep well overnight in the refrigerator.

*Variation:* omit the kidney beans and use the same quantity of chick peas.

*FROM THE TOP: Deep-dish salad bowl; Red bean salad*

## CRACKED WHEAT SALAD

SERVES 2
*100 g (4 oz) bulgur wheat*
*300 ml (½ pint) boiling water*
*2 tablespoons lemon juice*
*1 tablespoon olive oil*
*4 tablespoons chopped fresh parsley*
*4 tablespoons chopped spring onion*
*2 tablespoons chopped fresh mint*
*2 tomatoes, skinned and finely chopped*
*salt*
*freshly ground black pepper*
*4 lettuce leaves (optional)*

To garnish:
*lemon twists*
*sprigs of mint*

**Preparation time:** 30 minutes

V Suitable for vegans

This is a substantial Middle Eastern salad based on wheat which has been cracked and steamed. This wheat, called bulgur or burghul wheat, can be bought at health-food shops.

There is a large quantity of parsley and mint in the salad; they are used rather like a vegetable, and the more you put in the better. In the winter, when it's difficult to get fresh herbs, try using chopped watercress instead. Cracked wheat salad makes a useful addition to a supper buffet along with other contrasting salads, such as a tomato salad and a cucumber and yogurt salad.

1. Put the wheat into a bowl and cover with boiling water. Leave for 10–15 minutes, until the wheat has absorbed all the water and puffed up.
2. Add the lemon juice, oil, chopped parsley, spring onion, mint and tomato. Mix well and season to taste.
3. Garnish with the lemon twists and sprigs of mint. This salad looks most attractive on a bed of lettuce; to serve it this way, put two lettuce leaves on two serving plates or in one large bowl, then spoon the salad mixture into the lettuce leaves.

## CHUNKY SALAD

*1 large lettuce with a firm heart, such as iceberg, or 2 small lettuces with firm hearts, such as sugar cos*
*4 firm tomatoes, washed and cut into quarters or smaller*
*½ cucumber, washed and cut into chunky pieces*
*8 spring onions, chopped*

**Preparation time:** 5 minutes

V Suitable for vegans

1. Cut the lettuce into chunky pieces, then wash these carefully under running water, keeping the pieces as intact as possible. Shake well.
2. Put the lettuce chunks into a bowl with the tomatoes, cucumber and onions.

## TOMATO AND ONION SALAD

SERVES 6
*750 g (1½ lb) tomatoes, peeled and sliced*
*2 onions, peeled and thinly sliced*
*2 tablespoons olive oil*
*salt*
*freshly ground black pepper*
*sprig of parsley, to garnish*

**Preparation time:** 5 minutes

V Suitable for vegans

1. Put the tomatoes and onions into a shallow dish, mixing them together.
2. Pour the oil over them, making sure it's well distributed. Season with salt and pepper. This salad is best made an hour or so in advance and stirred several times. Add the garnish just before serving.

*CLOCKWISE FROM TOP LEFT: Chunky salad; Cracked wheat salad; Tomato and onion salad*

# CAULIFLOWER AND APPLE SALAD

350 g (12 oz) cauliflower florets
1 dessert apple, washed, cored and sliced
2 tomatoes, washed and chopped
2 carrots, scraped and coarsely grated
sprigs of watercress, shredded
1–2 tablespoons lemon juice
50 g (2 oz) raisins
2 tablespoons olive oil (optional)
salt
freshly ground black pepper
sprig of parsley, to garnish

**Preparation time:** 10 minutes

Ｖ Suitable for vegans
1. Mix together all the salad ingredients, adding olive oil if you're using it. Season with salt and pepper. (The cauliflower florets may be lightly cooked in boiling, salted water for 2–3 minutes, if wished.) Garnish just before serving.

# CHICORY, ORANGE AND WATERCRESS SALAD

SERVES 2
2 heads of chicory, washed
½ bunch watercress
2 small oranges, peeled and cut into slices

Dressing:
50 g (2 oz) Danish blue or Roquefort cheese
4 tablespoons soured cream

**Preparation time:** 15 minutes

1. Arrange the chicory leaves and sprigs of watercress alternately in a circle with the leaf tips pointing outwards, like the spokes of a wheel, on a large serving dish or two individual plates.
2. Put the orange slices in the centre, also in a circular pattern.
3. Make the dressing by mixing together the cheese and soured cream. Pour the dressing into the centre of the salad over the orange.

# GRAPEFRUIT AND AVOCADO SALAD WITH MINTY DRESSING

2 avocado pears, halved, peeled and stones
    removed
2 grapefruits
2 oranges
½ teaspoon sugar
2 tablespoons olive oil
1 tablespoon chopped fresh mint
salt
freshly ground black pepper
6–10 frisé leaves, washed and torn into
    bite-sized pieces, or 2 heads of chicory,
    washed and leaves separated
sprig of mint, to garnish

**Preparation time:** 30 minutes

1. Cut the avocado pears into thin slices. Spread the slices out on a plate.
2. Holding a grapefruit over the plate, peel with a sharp knife. Use a sawing action, cutting down to the flesh and removing all the white pith. Then cut each segment of fruit away from the inner white skin.
3. When all the segments have been removed from the grapefruit, squeeze the remaining juice from the skin over the avocado pears. Repeat with the other citrus fruit, keeping the segments separately.
4. Turn the avocado pear slices in the juice, then drain off any excess juice into a small bowl, adding the sugar, olive oil, mint and seasoning to make a dressing.
5. To assemble the salad, cover four plates with frisé or chicory leaves, then arrange segments of grapefruit, orange and avocado on top, dividing them between the plates. Give the dressing a quick stir, then spoon a little over each salad and garnish.

*CLOGKWISE FROM TOP LEFT: Cauliflower and apple salad; Chicory, orange and watercress salad; Grapefruit and avocado salad with minty dressing*

## CHICORY, WALNUT AND WATERCRESS SALAD

*1 garlic clove, crushed*
*salt*
*freshly ground black pepper*
*1 tablespoon wine vinegar*
*3 tablespoons olive oil*
*4 heads of chicory, washed*
*1 large bunch watercress*
*50 g (2 oz) walnuts, roughly chopped*

**Preparation time:** 15 minutes

Y Suitable for vegans
1. Put the garlic into a salad bowl with some salt and pepper and the wine vinegar. Mix together, then add the oil.
2. Break the chicory into even-sized pieces and add these to the bowl, together with the watercress and walnuts.

3. Turn the salad gently with salad servers so that everything gets evenly coated with the dressing. Check the seasoning and serve immediately.

## BEAN SPROUT AND RED PEPPER SALAD

*350 g (12 oz) carton beansprouts, washed*
*1 red pepper, seeded and chopped*
*1 small onion, peeled and sliced*
*1 large carrot, scraped and coarsely grated*
*sprig of parsley, to garnish*

Dressing:
*1 teaspoon sugar*
*2 teaspoons Dijon mustard*
*1 tablespoon wine vinegar*
*1 tablespoon soy sauce*
*2 tablespoons olive oil*
*salt*
*freshly ground black pepper*

**Preparation time:** 10 minutes

Y Suitable for vegans
1. Put all the vegetables into a bowl.
2. To make the dressing, mix together the first four ingredients, then gradually beat in the oil and season to taste with salt and pepper. Toss with the vegetable mixture before serving.

## CREAMY COLESLAW

SERVES 8
*450 g (1 lb) white cabbage, finely shredded*
*225 g (8 oz) carrots, scraped and coarsely grated*
*2 onions, peeled and finely chopped*
*100 g (4 oz) raisins*

Dressing:
*1 teaspoon dry mustard*
*150 ml (¼ pint) soured cream*
*salt*
*freshly ground black pepper*

**Preparation time:** 15 minutes

1. Put the cabbage, carrots, onions and raisins into a large bowl.
2. In a small bowl, blend the mustard with the soured cream, and season with salt and pepper. Add this to the salad, mixing well.

*Variation:* try a spicy yogurt dressing. In a small bowl, beat together 150 ml (¼ pint) thick Greek yogurt, 1 teaspoon ground turmeric and 1 clove garlic, crushed.

*FROM THE TOP: Chicory, walnut and watercress salad; Beansprout and red pepper salad; Creamy coleslaw*

# CONFETTI SALAD

**SERVES 10**

2 tablespoons Dijon mustard
2 tablespoons wine vinegar
8 tablespoons olive oil
salt
freshly ground black pepper
4 large carrots, scraped and coarsely grated
450 g (1 lb) white cabbage, finely shredded
450 g (1 lb) red cabbage, finely shredded
tender sticks from 1 head of celery, sliced
1 red pepper, seeded and finely chopped
1 green pepper, seeded and finely chopped

**Preparation time:** 15 minutes

V Suitable for vegans

This is a particularly pretty salad, with crisp textures. It is an excellent choice when entertaining on a grand scale as it can be made well in advance; it is also an easy salad to transport to picnics. Cover with clingfilm and store in the refrigerator until required.

1. Put the mustard into a large bowl and stir in the vinegar, oil and some salt and pepper, to make a dressing.

2. Add all the prepared vegetables and mix well. This can be made several hours in advance.

# CRUNCHY CABBAGE AND APPLE SALAD

**SERVES 6–8**

450 g (1 lb) white cabbage, finely shredded
2 apples, cored and diced
2 cooked beetroots, skinned and diced
2 celery sticks, chopped
6 spring onions, sliced
few drops of lemon juice
salt
freshly ground black pepper

To serve:
few leaves of radicchio, washed

**Preparation time:** 10 minutes

V Suitable for vegans

1. Put all the salad ingredients into a bowl and mix together. Season with a little salt and pepper. Place the radicchio in a deep serving bowl and spoon the cabbage salad into the leaves. Do not make this salad too far in advance, otherwise the beetroot will bleed over the apples and cabbage.

# CARROT, BANANA AND PECAN SALAD

**SERVES 2**

2 bananas, peeled and sliced
1 large carrot, coarsely grated
3 tablespoons soured cream or thick plain
    yogurt
1 tablespoon unsweetened desiccated coconut
½ bunch watercress
25 g (1 oz) pecans, chopped

**Preparation time:** 10 minutes

This is a delicious combination of flavours and textures and is popular with people who do not like the usual salad mixtures. The pecans give a delicious flavour but you can omit these and use walnuts or chopped almonds, if you prefer. For an alternative dressing, try using mayonnaise, either alone or mixed half and half with plain yogurt. For a slimmer's version, simply toss the salad in a little orange juice to preserve the colour of the banana.

1. Mix together the bananas, carrot, soured cream and coconut. Spoon the mixture into the centre of one large or two individual bowls, then arrange the watercress round the edge. Sprinkle the nuts on top of the banana mixture.

*CLOCKWISE FROM THE TOP: Confetti salad; Crunchy cabbage and apple salad; Carrot, banana and pecan salad*

# CHEESE, TOMATO AND PEPPER SALAD WITH HONEY AND MUSTARD DRESSING

4–6 lettuce leaves
4 tomatoes, skinned and sliced
100 g (4 oz) vegetarian Cheddar-type
    cheese, finely diced
½ red pepper, seeded and finely diced
½ green pepper, seeded and finely diced
½ yellow pepper, seeded and finely diced,
    or 1 carrot, scraped and finely diced

Dressing:
½ teaspoon mustard powder
1 tablespoon clear honey
2 tablespoons wine vinegar
2 tablespoons olive oil
salt
freshly ground black pepper

**Preparation time:** 20 minutes

A pleasant combination of flavours and textures with a creamy, tangy dressing, this salad also makes a good first course.
1. Arrange the lettuce on four individual serving plates or in one large bowl. Place the tomatoes in a circle on top of the lettuce, and the cheese in a pile in the centre. Arrange the peppers or peppers and carrot round the plates or bowl.
2. To make the dressing, blend the mustard powder with the honey until smooth, then gradually add the vinegar, then the oil. Season to taste, mix well. Serve separately in a small jug.

*Most hard cheeses contain a small quantity of rennet (1 part rennet to 5000 parts milk). Rennet is a digestive juice taken from the stomachs of calves which means that most cheeses are not 100% vegetarian. Now it is possible to buy excellent vegetarian cheeses; most supermarkets stock Cheddar and a wider range is available from health food shops. Some soft white cheeses include rennet, but some do not. Ask for information when you buy, or contact the manufacturers.*

# GREEK SALAD

SERVES 2
1 medium onion, peeled and sliced
1 tablespoon olive oil
1 tablespoon wine vinegar
salt
freshly ground black pepper
4 tomatoes, thinly sliced
½ cucumber, peeled and chopped
10–12 black olives
100 g (4 oz) feta cheese or other white,
    crumbly cheese, diced
chopped fresh parsley, to garnish

**Preparation time:** 10 minutes, plus standing

1. Put the onion into a bowl with the oil, vinegar and a little salt and pepper; mix well, then leave to stand for 30–60 minutes, if possible, to allow the onion to soften slightly. Stir occasionally.
2. Add the tomatoes, cucumber, olives and cheese, mixing gently to distribute all the ingredients. Serve sprinkled with the chopped parsley.

*FROM THE LEFT: Greek salad; Cheese, tomato and pepper salad with Honey and mustard dressing*

## COLOURFUL CABBAGE SALAD

350 g (12 oz) white cabbage, shredded
2 carrots, scraped and coarsely grated
2 tomatoes, skinned and chopped
2 celery sticks, diced
1 red pepper, seeded and finely chopped
4 spring onions, chopped
2 tablespoons olive oil
2 tablespoons red wine vinegar
4 tablespoons raisins
salt
freshly ground black pepper
roasted cashew nuts, to garnish

**Preparation time:** 15 minutes

Ⓥ Suitable for vegans
Red cabbage can also be used in this recipe either totally replacing the white cabbage or mixing it half and half. For an extra creamy dressing whisk 2 tablespoons of thick plain yogurt into the oil and vinegar.
1. Put all the ingredients into a bowl and mix together well. Garnish with the roasted cashew nuts.

## TWO-BEAN SALAD IN RADICCHIO

225 g (8 oz) frozen broad beans
225 g (8 oz) fresh or frozen French beans
1 tablespoon red wine vinegar
3 tablespoons olive oil
salt
freshly ground black pepper
2 tablespoons chopped summer savory
2 medium-sized radicchio

**Preparation time:** 5 minutes
**Cooking time:** 5–10 minutes

Ⓥ Suitable for vegans
1. Cook the beans together in a little boiling water for 5–10 minutes. Drain well.
2. Put the vinegar and oil into a bowl and mix together, then add the hot beans, some salt and pepper and the chopped savory.
3. Mix well, then leave until cool. Arrange the radicchio leaves in a shallow serving dish and spoon over the bean mixture.

## STUFFED AVOCADO SALAD

SERVES 2
1 large ripe avocado pear, halved and stone removed
1 tablespoon lemon juice
2 tomatoes, skinned and chopped
2 spring onions, chopped
½ small green pepper, seeded and finely chopped
50 g (2 oz) vegetarian Cheddar-type cheese, grated
salt
freshly ground black pepper

To garnish:
4 lettuce leaves (optional)
few sprigs of parsley
twists of lemon

**Preparation time:** 15 minutes

1. Using a teaspoon, scoop out the avocado flesh, being careful not to damage the skin which will be needed for serving the salad.
2. Dice the flesh and place in a bowl with the lemon juice, tomatoes, spring onion, green pepper and cheese. Season to taste. Spoon the mixture into the avocado skins.
3. Arrange the stuffed avocados on the lettuce leaves, if liked, and garnish with sprigs of parsley and twists of lemon.

CLOCKWISE FROM THE TOP: Colourful cabbage salad; Two-bean salad with radicchio; Stuffed avocado salad

# PUDDINGS AND DESSERTS

**A** pudding or dessert rounds off a meal perfectly and this applies just as much to a vegetarian meal as to a meat one! Many popular desserts are suitable for vegetarians, as long as they do not contain animal suet or lard and a vegetable gelatine is used. Most vegetarians also prefer to use wholewheat flour and unrefined sugars or honey where possible. Here is a selection of recipes to complement vegetarian dishes.

*Raspberry and Pistachio Ice Cream (recipe, page 84)*

# PEARS POACHED IN HONEY WITH BRANDYSNAPS

**SERVES 6**

*6 ripe Conference pears*
*100 g (4 oz) clear honey*
*450 ml (¾ pint) water*
*sprigs of mint, to decorate*

Brandysnaps:

*50 g (2 oz) butter or margarine*
*50 g (2 oz) Barbados sugar*
*50 g (2 oz) golden syrup*
*50 g (2 oz) plain 85 per cent wholewheat flour*
*½ teaspoon ground ginger, or ground mixed spice*
*little grated lemon rind*
*150 ml (¼ pint) double cream, whipped, to finish (optional)*

**Preparation time:** 30 minutes
**Cooking time:** about 1 hour
**Oven:** 160°C, 325°F, Gas Mark 3

The brandysnaps can be made a day or two in advance and stored in an airtight tin until needed. Their crunchy texture makes a lovely contrast to the sweetness of the pears and the richness of the cream.

1. Peel the pears, keeping them whole and leaving on the stalks.

2. Put the honey and water in a fairly large saucepan and bring to the boil; boil for 2 minutes, then put in the pears. Bring back to the boil, then cover the saucepan and leave the pears to simmer gently for 30–40 minutes until soft right through to the centre.

3. Take the pears out of the saucepan using a slotted spoon and put them on a serving dish. Boil the honey and water mixture rapidly until it has reduced to about 3 tablespoons of glossy-looking syrup. Spoon this syrup over the pears, then leave them to cool.

4. Grease one or two large baking sheets. Stir the butter, sugar and syrup together in a pan over a gentle heat until melted. Remove from the heat and sift in the flour and ground ginger or ground mixed spice, and grate in a little lemon rind to taste.

5. Drop teaspoonfuls of the mixture on to a baking sheet, leaving plenty of room for the brandysnaps to spread; flatten lightly with a palette knife.

6. Bake in a preheated oven for 8–10 minutes, until evenly browned. Cool on the tray for 1–2 minutes, until just firm enough to handle, then loosen with a knife and quickly roll the brandysnaps round the greased handle of a wooden spoon, then carefully slide them off and leave them to cool. This process has to be done quickly or the brandysnaps will harden. If this happens, pop them back into the oven for a few minutes to soften and start again!

7. Serve the brandysnaps with the pears, decorated with sprigs of mint, either as they are, accompanied by a bowl of whipped cream, or, just before serving, use a piping bag with a star nozzle (or a teaspoon) to fill the brandysnaps with whipped cream.

# RASPBERRY AND PISTACHIO ICE CREAM

**SERVES 8**

*350 g (12 oz) fresh raspberries, washed*
*175 g (6 oz) sugar or honey*
*450 ml (¾ pint) whipping cream*
*100 g (4 oz) pistachio nuts, chopped*

**Preparation time:** 25 minutes

1. Blend, then sieve the raspberries to remove the pips and make a smooth purée. Add the sugar or honey.

2. Whip the cream until it is thick, then fold in the raspberry purée.

3. Pour the mixture into a plastic container and freeze until half-frozen, then stir well and add most of the pistachio nuts, reserving a few for decoration.

4. Return to the freezer and freeze until solid. Remove the ice cream from the freezer about 30 minutes before serving. Spoon into individual bowls and sprinkle with pistachio nuts.

*FROM THE TOP: Pears poached in honey with Brandysnaps; Raspberry and pistachio ice cream*

# BLACKBERRY FOOL

450 g (1 lb) fresh or frozen blackberries
100 g (4 oz) smooth low-fat white cheese
honey or sugar, to taste
150 ml (¼ pint) whipping cream, whipped
sprigs of mint, to decorate

**Preparation time:** 20 minutes, plus cooling

This simple, creamy fool can be made with other fruits instead of blackberries. Redcurrants are delicious; cook these as described and sieve them to remove stems and seeds. Strawberries and raspberries do not need to be cooked. For a lower fat version, use a carton of thick Greek yogurt instead of the cream.

This mixture can also be served like ice cream. Freeze the chilled mixture until firm. Soften in the refrigerator for 10–15 minutes before required.

1. Put the blackberries into a dry saucepan and heat gently until the juices run and the blackberries are tender. Remove from the heat and leave to cool.
2. Drain and reserve the juice from the blackberries and either purée and sieve the fruit for a smooth texture, or mash them.
3. Stir in the low-fat white cheese and enough of the reserved blackberry juice to make a creamy consistency.
4. Sweeten as necessary with sugar or honey, then fold in the whipped cream. Serve chilled, decorated with sprigs of mint.

# BANANA AND ALMOND CRUMBLE

4 bananas, peeled and sliced
100 g (4 oz) 100 per cent wholewheat flour
50 g (2 oz) ground almonds
4 tablespoons butter or margarine
50 g (2 oz) Barbados sugar
8 teaspoons flaked almonds, crushed
whipped cream, to serve

**Preparation time:** 5 minutes
**Cooking time:** about 15 minutes

1. Heat the grill. Put the bananas into a lightly greased, shallow ovenproof dish.
2. Mix together the flour, ground almonds and butter or margarine. Add the sugar and flaked almonds, then put this mixture over the bananas in an even layer.
3. Place under the grill for about 15 minutes, until the crumble is crisp and lightly browned. Serve with whipped cream.

# MANGO SORBET WITH HONEY AND CARDAMOM SAUCE

2 large ripe mangoes, halved, peeled and
    stones removed and flesh cut into even-
    sized chunks
2 egg whites

Sauce:
1 teaspoon cardamom pods
3 tablespoons clear honey
3 tablespoons orange juice

To decorate:
slices of mango
few pistachio nuts, shelled and chopped

**Preparation time:** 35 minutes, plus cooling

1. Blend the mango flesh which should make about 600 ml (1 pint) of purée. Put this into a polythene container and freeze until firm round the edges.
2. Whisk the egg whites until stiff. Add the cold mango purée to the egg whites a little at a time, continuing to whisk. Return to the freezer and freeze until firm.
3. Meanwhile make the sauce. Crush the cardamom pods and remove the black seeds. Crush the seeds as finely as you can. Then mix them with the honey and orange juice. Cover and leave for at least 30 minutes for the flavours to blend.
4. Just before serving, strain the sauce. Remove the sorbet from the freezer 30 minutes before it is required. Serve in individual bowls with some slices of mango, the sauce and a few pistachio nuts.

*CLOKWISE FROM TOP LEFT: Blackberry fool;
Banana and almond crumble; Mango sorbet with
Honey and cardamom sauce*

# PEACH AND RATAFIA TRIFLE

SERVES 6–8

*225 g (8 oz) ratafias, lightly crushed*
*2 tablespoons raspberry jam*
*6 tablespoons sweet white wine*
*4 white peaches, skinned and sliced and*
*    brushed with lemon juice*
*300 ml (½ pint) whipping cream*
*2–3 tablespoons caster sugar*
*25 g (1 oz) slithered almonds*
*sprigs of mint, to decorate*

**Preparation time:** 15 minutes, plus chilling

1. Mix the ratafias with the jam and 4 tablespoons of the white wine. Divide the mixture between 6–8 individual serving dishes, then place the peaches on top.
2. Whip the cream with the caster sugar and the remaining white wine, then spoon this on top of the peaches.

3. Arrange the almonds on top of the cream mixture, then chill for at least 30 minutes. Decorate with sprigs of mint and serve.

# HAZELNUT MERINGUES WITH CHOCOLATE SAUCE

MAKES 6 PAIRS

*butter or oil for greasing*
*flour for sprinkling*
*2 egg whites*
*pinch of cream of tartar*
*100 g (4 oz) Demerara sugar*
*50 g (2 oz) hazelnuts, roasted and ground*
*300 ml (½ pint) whipping cream*

*Sauce:*
*225 g (8 oz) milk chocolate*
*150 ml (¼ pint) milk*

**Preparation time:** 45 minutes
**Cooking time:** 1½–2 hours
**Oven:** 150°C, 300°F, Gas Mark 2:
    then 110°C, 225°F, Gas Mark ¼

1. Line a baking tray with a piece of greaseproof paper, grease with butter or cooking oil and sprinkle with flour.
2. Put the egg whites into a clean, grease-free bowl with the cream of tartar and whisk until stiff and dry. You should be able to turn the bowl upside down without spilling the egg white. Then gradually whisk in the sugar. Carefully fold in the hazelnuts.
3. Drop spoonfuls of the mixture on to the prepared baking sheet, making 12 meringues.
4. Put the meringues into the preheated oven, then reduce the oven temperature. Bake for 1½–2 hours, until they are crisp. Turn off the heat and leave the meringues to cool in the oven.
5. Remove them from the baking tray with a palette knife; while the meringues are cooking, make the sauce.
6. Put the chocolate into a small saucepan with the milk and heat gently until the chocolate has melted. Remove from the

heat, pour into a serving jug and leave to cool.
7. Whip the cream and use this to sandwich the meringues together in pairs. Serve with the sauce.

*FROM THE TOP: Peach and ratafia trifle; Hazelnut meringues with chocolate sauce*

# BLACKCURRANT RIPPLE

*oil for brushing*
*3 egg whites*
*75 g (3 oz) demerara sugar*
*450 g (1 lb) fresh or frozen blackcurrants*
*extra sugar, to taste*
*300 ml (½ pint) whipping cream*

**Preparation time:** 30 minutes
**Cooking time:** 2–3 hours
**Oven:** 110°C, 225°F, Gas Mark ¼

This is a useful ice cream because it can be served straight from the freezer, without softening. For this recipe the meringues are made with less sugar than usual.

Make sure that the serving dish you use is not a metal one. The acidity of the blackcurrants combined with the metal would taint the mixture.

1. Line a large baking tray with grease-proof paper and brush with oil.
2. Whisk the egg whites until very stiff, then whisk in half the sugar and fold in the rest. Put spoonfuls of the mixture on to the baking tray, then bake the meringues in a preheated oven for 2–3 hours, until dried out and crisp.
3. Meanwhile, prepare the blackcurrant purée. Put the blackcurrants into a saucepan and cook gently, without added water, for about 10 minutes, until the juices run and the blackcurrants are tender.
4. Liquidize, then sieve the blackcurrants. Sweeten the purée to taste. Cool.
5. To complete the mixture, whisk the cream until standing in soft peaks, adding a little sugar to taste.
6. Break the meringues into rough pieces, not too small, and fold these into the cream, together with the blackcurrant purée, to create a ripple effect. Spoon the mixture into a serving dish and freeze until firm.

# PEAR AND GINGER PIE

*225 g (8 oz) plain 85 or 100 per cent*
    *wholewheat flour*
*100 g (4 oz) butter or margarine*
*3 tablespoons cold water*
*milk, to glaze*

Filling:
*1 teaspoon ground ginger*
*750 g (1½ lb) ripe dessert pears, peeled, cored*
    *and sliced*
*2 tablespoons Barbados sugar*

**Preparation time:** 40 minutes
**Cooking time:** 30 minutes
**Oven:** 200°C, 400°F, Gas Mark 6

This is a pleasant change from the classic apple pie, but you could replace the pears with the same quantity of cooking apples.
1. Sift the flour into a bowl, adding the bran left behind in the sieve, too. Rub in the fat with your fingertips until the mixture looks like breadcrumbs, then mix in the water to make a dough.
2. Roll out half of the pastry on a floured board and use to line a 20–23 cm (8–9 inch) pie plate.
3. Sprinkle the ginger over the pastry, making sure that it's well distributed, then put the pears on top of the pastry and sprinkle with the sugar. Roll out the rest of the pastry and use it to make a crust for the pie. Trim the pastry and crimp the edges of the pie with a fork. Make two or three holes for steam to escape and brush with milk.
4. Bake in a preheated oven for about 30 minutes, until the pastry is crisp and lightly browned. If the pears make a great deal of liquid, simply pour this off after you have cut the first slice of pie.

*FROM THE TOP: Blackcurrant ripple; Pear and ginger pie*

## MELBA PEACHES

SERVES 2

*2 ripe peaches*
*225 g (8 oz) fresh or frozen raspberries*
*1 tablespoon fruit sugar*
*sprigs of mint, to decorate*

**Preparation time:** 15 minutes

Y Suitable for vegans

1. Put the peaches into a bowl, cover with boiling water and leave for 2 minutes. Drain and peel. Cut the peaches in half and remove the stones.

2. Reserve 6 raspberries for decoration and purée the rest with the fruit sugar in a blender. Sieve into a bowl.

3. Put two peach halves, cavity side down, on each plate. Spoon the raspberry mixture over the peach halves and decorate with the mint and the reserved raspberries.

## GRAPE CHEESECAKE

SERVES 6–8

*175 g (6 oz) semi-sweet wholewheat biscuits,*
  *finely crushed*
*75 g (3 oz) butter or margarine, melted*

Filling:
*450 g (1 lb) curd or cream cheese*
*150 ml (5 fl oz) plain thick yogurt*
*4 tablespoons clear honey*
*50 g (2 oz) Demerara sugar*
*4 eggs*
*2 tablespoons ground almonds*
*1 teaspoon vanilla extract or essence*

Topping:
*150 ml (¼ pint) soured cream*
*100 g (4 oz) black grapes, halved and seeded*
*100 g (4 oz) green grapes, halved and seeded*
*3 tablespoons clear honey*

**Preparation time:** 40 minutes
**Cooking time:** 1¼–1½ hours
**Oven:** 160°C, 325°F, Gas Mark 3

1. First make the crumb crust. Mix together the biscuit crumbs and melted butter or margarine. Spoon this mixture into the bottom of a 20 cm (8 inch) loose-bottom or spring-clip flan tin. Press the crumb crust down firmly.

2. Next, make the filling. Put all the ingredients into a bowl and beat together until smooth and creamy. Pour this mixture on to the crumb crust and spread evenly.

3. Bake the cheesecake for 1¼–1½ hours in a preheated oven until firm in the centre. Remove the cheesecake from the oven and carefully spoon the soured cream on top, gently levelling it with a knife.

4. Turn off the heat but put the cheesecake back in the still-warm oven for 15–20 minutes, then leave to cool.

5. When completely cold, gently release the sides of the tin and lift the cheesecake on to a serving plate. Arrange the grapes on top in circles of alternating colours.

6. Put the honey into a small saucepan and heat, to make it more liquid, then spoon or brush this over the grapes. Cool.

*FROM THE TOP: Melba peaches; Grape cheesecake*

# FRUIT SALAD

*2 oranges*
*175 g (6 oz) strawberries, hulled and washed*
*225 g (8 oz) black grapes, halved and seeded*
*2 kiwi fruit, peeled and sliced*
*2 apples, cored and sliced (unpeeled if the*
*   skins are good)*
*150 ml (¼ pint) orange juice*
*sprigs of mint, to decorate*

**Preparation time:** 20 minutes

Y Suitable for vegans
1. Holding the oranges over a bowl and using a sharp knife, cut away the peel and white pith, using a sawing action and cutting round the fruit as if peeling an apple to produce a long piece of peel.

Then cut the segments away from the white inner skin.
2. Put the oranges into the bowl and add the rest of the fruit and the orange juice. Spoon into individual glass dishes and decorate with sprigs of mint.

# CHOCOLATE ROULADE

SERVES 6
*5 eggs, separated*
*175 g (6 oz) soft brown sugar*
*3 tablespoons hot water*
*175 g (6 oz) plain chocolate, melted*

Filling:
*300 ml (½ pint) whipping cream, whipped*

To finish:
*icing sugar*
*chocolate leaves*

**Preparation time:** 45 minutes, plus cooling
**Cooking time:** 15 minutes
**Oven:** 200°C, 400°F, Gas Mark 6

1. Grease a 25 x 35 cm (10 x 14 inch) Swiss roll tin and line with a piece of greased greaseproof paper.
2. Put the egg yolks into a bowl with the sugar and whisk until thick and pale. Mix the hot water with the melted chocolate, then gently stir this into the egg yolk mixture.
3. Whisk the egg whites until stiff, then fold these gently into the mixture. Pour the mixture into the tin, quickly spreading it out to the edges. Bake in a preheated oven for 15 minutes until well risen and just firm to the touch.

4. Cool the mixture in the tin for 10 minutes, then cover with a damp teacloth and leave for 10 minutes or overnight.
5. Remove the cloth, and turn the cake out on to a piece of greaseproof paper that has been generously dusted with icing sugar. Carefully remove the greaseproof paper from the top of the cake, then leave it to cool completely. When it is cold, trim the edges and spread the whole cake evenly with the whipped cream. Carefully roll the cake up, using the paper to help; don't worry if it cracks! Sprinkle with more icing sugar.
6. This roulade will keep well in the refrigerator for several hours, and can also be frozen successfully. Serve on a large plate decorated with the chocolate leaves or other chocolate decoration.

*FROM THE TOP: Fruit salad; Chocolate roulade*

# CHOCOLATE RUM TRUFFLES

MAKES 18
*100 g (4 oz) plain chocolate*
*150 ml (¼ pint) double cream*
*1 tablespoon rum*

To finish:
*cocoa powder for coating*
*small bon-bon cases, if available*

**Preparation time:** 20 minutes, plus chilling
**Cooking time:** 10 minutes

1. Break the chocolate into pieces and put into a small saucepan with the double cream.
2. Heat very gently until the chocolate has melted, then remove from the heat, scrape into a bowl and leave to cool.
3. Add the rum to the cream and chocolate mixture and whisk thoroughly until paler in colour and fluffy. Place in the refrigerator until firm enough to handle.
4. Sprinkle some cocoa powder over a plate, then place heaped teaspoonfuls of the chocolate mixture on this, and sprinkle with more cocoa powder.
5. Quickly roll each piece of mixture in the cocoa powder to make a truffle, then place in a bon-bon case or on a small serving dish. Chill until ready to serve.

# VEGETARIAN CHRISTMAS PUDDING WITH BRANDY BUTTER

SERVES 8
*225 g (8 oz) currants*
*100 g (4 oz) raisins*
*100 g (4 oz) sultanas*
*100 g (4 oz) chopped candied peel*
*25 g (1 oz) almonds, skinned and chopped*
*100 g (4 oz) plain 85 or 100 per cent*
    *wholewheat flour*
*½ teaspoon salt*
*½ teaspoon grated nutmeg*
*½ teaspoon ground ginger*
*1½ teaspoons ground mixed spice*
*225 g (8 oz) Barbados sugar*
*100 g (4 oz) fresh wholewheat breadcrumbs*
*225 g (8 oz) hard butter or vegetable suet,*
    *coarsely grated*
*rind and juice of 1 lemon*
*2 eggs*
*1 tablespoon treacle*
*about 4 tablespoons milk, or milk and rum*
    *mixed*
*4 tablespoons brandy*
*sprig of holly, to decorate*

Brandy butter:
*100 g (4 oz) light brown sugar*
*rum or brandy*
*100 g (4 oz) unsalted butter, softened*

**Preparation time:** 1 hour
**Cooking time:** 4 hours, plus 3 hours reheating

In this pudding, butter or a hard white vegetable suet replace the traditional suet. The pudding tastes just as good, and has a deliciously spicy flavour. It can be made up to two months in advance and will keep well (and mature) in a cool, dry place.
1. Grease a 1.2 litre (2 pint) pudding basin and have ready a saucepan which is large enough to hold the pudding basin. Wash the currants, raisins and sultanas in warm water, then pat dry on paper towels.
2. Put the fruit into a large bowl with the candied peel and almonds. Sift the flour, salt and spices into the bowl on top of the fruit, then add the sugar, breadcrumbs and butter or vegetable suet.
3. Mix well, then stir in the lemon rind and juice, eggs, treacle and enough of the milk or milk and rum to make a soft mixture which will fall heavily from the spoon when you shake it. Spoon the mixture into the pudding basin, cover with a piece of greaseproof paper and then overwrap with foil, and secure.
4. Put the basin into the saucepan and pour in enough water to come half-way up the pudding bowl. Bring to the boil, then cover the saucepan and leave the pudding to steam gently for 4 hours. Watch the water-level in the saucepan and top up with some boiling water from time to time.
5. Leave to cool, then wrap the pudding in fresh greaseproof paper and overwrap with foil. Store it in a cool dry place.
6. Steam the pudding again for 3 hours before eating, then turn it out on to a warm serving plate and flame with brandy. To do this, put 4 tablespoons of brandy into a metal soup ladle and warm by holding over a gas flame or electric ring, then quickly ignite the brandy and pour over and round the pudding. Decorate with a sprig of holly.
7. This pudding is delicious with whipped cream, or a brandy or rum butter, made by beating light brown sugar and enough rum or brandy to flavour, into soft, unsalted butter. This can be made well in advance, and frozen.

*FROM THE TOP: Chocolate rum truffles; Vegetarian Christmas pudding with Brandy butter*

# BREAD, CAKES AND BISCUITS

**B**aking your own bread, cakes and biscuits is one of the most satisfying activities. The results are wholesome, mouthwatering to look at, delicious to eat and the kitchen is filled with a warm, welcoming aroma. In this section you'll find a range of recipes which make use of wholewheat flour, vegetable fats and, usually, unrefined sugars, and they will all guarantee your popularity!

*Flower Cakes (recipe, page 102)*

## QUICK WHOLEWHEAT ROLLS

MAKES 8–10 ROLLS
*150 ml (¼ pint) milk*
*150 ml (¼ pint) water*
*50 g (2 oz) butter or margarine*
*225 g (8 oz) plain 85% wholewheat flour*
*225 g (8 oz) unbleached white flour*
*1 teaspoon salt*
*1 teaspoon sugar*
*10 g (¼ oz) packet of easy-blend yeast*

**Preparation time:** 35 minutes, plus proving
**Cooking time:** 15–20 minutes
**Oven:** 220°C, 425°F, Gas Mark 7

1. Heat together the milk, water and fat gently until the fat has melted. Cool to tepid.
2. Put the flours into a large bowl with the salt, sugar and yeast; add the milk mixture.
3. Mix to a dough, then knead for 5 minutes. Put the dough into a clean, lightly-oiled bowl, cover with clingfilm, and leave in a warm place for about 1 hour, until doubled in bulk.

4. Knock back the dough with your fist, then knead it again for 1–2 minutes.
5. Shape into 8–10 rolls and place well apart on a floured baking tray. Cover and leave in a warm place for 15–20 minutes. Bake in a preheated oven for 15–20 minutes. Serve warm.

## QUICK AND EASY BREAD

MAKES TWO 450 g (1 lb) LOAVES
*450 g (1 lb) plain 100 per cent wholewheat flour*
*2 teaspoons salt*
*2 packets instant dried yeast*
*1 x 25 mg tablet ascorbic acid (vitamin C) (optional)*
*1 tablespoon honey, molasses or black treacle*
*about 350 ml (12 fl oz) tepid water*

**Preparation time:** 15 minutes, plus proving
**Cooking time:** 35 minutes
**Oven:** 230°C, 450°F, Gas Mark 8

**V** Suitable for vegans
This is a quick bread to make, and adding the ascorbic acid speeds it up even more because it helps to accelerate fermentation. The finished bread has a light, moist, open texture.

You do need to use real 100 per cent wholewheat flour for this recipe as it doesn't work properly with other types of flour. For a wholesome, country look you can sprinkle the loaves with kibbled wheat (from healthfood shops) before baking.
1. Grease two 450 g (1 lb) bread tins thoroughly with butter. Put the flour, salt and yeast into a large bowl.
2. Crush the ascorbic acid tablet, then mix it with the honey, molasses or treacle and the water and stir well, then add this to the flour. Mix well to make a dough that is just too soft to knead.

3. Divide the dough in half and place one half in each tin. Cover the tins loosely with oiled clingfilm and leave in a warm place – or on the kitchen working surface – until the dough has risen by one-third. This will take 30–45 minutes, depending on the temperature.
4. Fifteen minutes or so before the dough is ready, preheat the oven. Bake the bread for 35 minutes, covering the loaves with a piece of foil after about 20 minutes.
5. Turn the loaves out of their tins and put them on a wire rack to cool.

*FROM THE TOP: Quick and easy bread; Quick wholewheat rolls*

# FLOWER CAKES

MAKES ABOUT 32
*1 quantity sponge mixture (page 120)*
*about 32 paper cake cases*

To decorate:
*500 g (1¼ lb) sifted icing sugar*
*7–8 tablespoons water*
*cake colourings to tone with sugar flowers*
*about 50 sugar flower cake decorations*

**Preparation time:** 20 minutes
**Cooking time:** 10–15 minutes
**Oven:** 190°C, 375°F, Gas Mark 5

Buy the biggest and prettiest icing sugar flower decorations you can find; or, better still, if you've the time and skill, make your own in soft pastel colours.
1. Make the cake mixture as described in the Clown cake recipe on page 120.
2. Put heaped teaspoonfuls into the paper cake cases and place on a baking tray.

3. Bake in a preheated oven for 10–15 minutes, until the cakes spring back when touched lightly in the centre. Cool on a wire rack.
4. Make the icing by mixing the icing sugar with the water; divide the mixture into 3 or 4 portions and colour each portion delicately to tone with the flowers.
5. Pour a little icing on to the top of each cake and spread lightly to the edges with a palette knife. Place a sugar flower in the centre of each cake.

# VEGETARIAN MINCE PIES

MAKES 36
*100 g (4 oz) currants*
*100 g (4 oz) raisins*
*100 g (4 oz) sultanas*
*50 g (2 oz) cooking dates (not sugar rolled)*
*50 g (2 oz) candied peel*
*50 g (2 oz) glacé cherries*
*50 g (2 oz) flaked almonds*
*1 ripe banana, peeled*
*4 tablespoons brandy or whisky*
*½ teaspoon each ground ginger, grated*
*nutmeg, ground mixed spice*
*caster sugar, to serve*

Pastry:
*750 g (1½ lb) plain 85 per cent wholewheat*
*flour*
*pinch of salt*
*350 g (12 oz) butter or margarine*
*6 tablespoons cold water*

**Preparation time:** 30 minutes
**Cooking time:** about 10 minutes
**Oven:** 200°C, 400°F, Gas Mark 6

This mincemeat relies on the fruit for sweetness, without added sugar, and it doesn't contain any fat. It tastes excellent and can be stored for a week in a covered bowl in the refrigerator, but doesn't keep in the same way as ordinary mincemeat because of the lack of added sugar, which acts as a preservative. This quantity of mincemeat will make 36 mince pies.
1. To make the mincemeat, simply mix everything together. You can do this in a food processor (which will chop the fruit, making a smoother texture), or by hand.
2. Lightly grease a shallow bun or muffin tin. Sift the flour and salt into a bowl, add the butter or margarine, and rub into the flour with your fingertips until the mixture resembles breadcrumbs.
3. Add the water, then press the mixture together to make a dough. Roll the dough out on a lightly floured board, then cut out 12 cm (4¾ inch) circles and 10 cm (4 inch) circles using round cutters.
4. Press one of the larger circles gently into each section of the bun or muffin tin, then

put a heaped teaspoon of mincemeat into each and cover with the smaller pastry circles.
5. Press down firmly at the edges, make a hole in the top for steam to escape, then bake in a preheated oven for about 10 minutes, until the pastry is lightly browned. Cool in the tin. Serve warm, sprinkled with caster sugar.

*FROM THE TOP: Flower cakes; Vegetarian mince pies*

# WHOLEWHEAT JAM TARTS

**MAKES 12**
*butter for greasing*
*100 g (4 oz) plain 100 per cent wholewheat flour*
*50 g (2 oz) butter or margarine*
*6 teaspoons cold water*

*Filling:*
*4 heaped tablespoons jam (preferably reduced sugar)*

**Preparation time:** 25 minutes
**Cooking time:** 10 minutes
**Oven:** 190°C, 375°F, Gas Mark 5

1. Grease a shallow bun or muffin tin. Put the flour into a bowl; add the fat, then rub it in with your fingertips until the mixture looks like breadcrumbs. Add the water, pressing the mixture together to form a dough.
2. Roll the pastry out carefully on a lightly floured board, then cut out 12 circles using a 6 cm (2½ inch) cutter. Press a pastry circle lightly into each cavity in the bun or muffin tin, then put a heaped teaspoonful of jam on to each one.
3. Bake the jam tarts near the top of a preheated oven for about 10 minutes, until the pastry is lightly browned. Cool in the tin.

# OATCAKES

**MAKES 20–22**
*225 g (8 oz) medium oatmeal*
*1 teaspoon salt*
*15 g (½ oz) butter or margarine*
*100 ml (3½ fl oz) tepid water*
*extra oatmeal for rolling out*

**Preparation time:** 25 minutes
**Cooking time:** 20 minutes
**Oven:** 180°C, 350°F, Gas Mark 4

Home-made oatcakes are delicious and easy to make. Make sure the oatmeal is really fresh, with no hint of a stale smell.
1. Put the oatmeal and salt into a bowl and rub in the butter or margarine. Add the water, mix, then leave for 5–10 minutes for the oatmeal to absorb the water.
2. Gather the mixture together and put it on a board that has been sprinkled with oatmeal.
3. Roll out the mixture to a depth of about 3 mm (⅛ inch) using plenty of oatmeal to prevent sticking, then cut into rounds using a 7.5 cm (3 inch) round cutter.
4. Place the rounds on a dry baking tray and bake for 15 minutes, then turn the oatcakes over and bake for a further 5 minutes. Cool on a wire rack.

# DATE SQUARES

**MAKES 16**
*100 g (4 oz) self-raising 100 per cent wholewheat flour*
*100 g (4 oz) rolled oats*
*100 g (4 oz) butter or margarine*
*50 g (2 oz) Barbados sugar*

*Filling:*
*225 g (8 oz) cooking dates (not sugar-rolled)*
*5 tablespoons water*
*½ teaspoon vanilla extract or essence*

**Preparation time:** 30 minutes
**Cooking time:** 30 minutes
**Oven:** 180°C, 350°F, Gas Mark 4

A sweet date filling sandwiched in a crumbly, oaty pastry.
1. Grease an 18 cm (7 inch) square tin. First prepare the filling: chop the dates roughly, removing any stones. Put them into a small saucepan with the water and heat gently for about 10 minutes, stirring often, until softened. Add the vanilla, then beat the dates with a wooden spoon to make a thick purée. Set aside to cool.
2. Put the flour and oats into a bowl; add the fat, rubbing it in with your fingertips until the mixture looks like breadcrumbs. Mix in the sugar.
3. Press half the mixture into the greased tin, then spread the cooled date mixture on top. Sprinkle the rest of the flour and oat mixture over the date mixture and press down with the back of a spoon. Bake in a preheated oven for 30 minutes. Mark into squares, then leave to cool in the tin.

*FROM THE LEFT: Date squares; Oatcakes; Wholewheat jam tarts*

# LITTLE BROWN SUGAR CHOCOLATE BUNS

MAKES 12

*175 g (6 oz) self-raising 85 per cent*
  *wholewheat flour*
*1 tablespoon cocoa powder*
*100 g (4 oz) soft butter or margarine*
*100 g (4 oz) Barbados sugar*
*2 eggs*
*few drops of vanilla extract or essence*
*12 paper cake cases*

Topping:
*100 g (4 oz) chocolate, melted*

**Preparation time:** 20 minutes
**Cooking time:** 15–20 minutes
**Oven:** 190°C, 375°F, Gas Mark 5

A variation is to use carob powder instead of cocoa, and a carob bar instead of chocolate, both available from healthfood shops.
1. Sift the flour and cocoa power into a bowl, then add the butter or margarine, sugar, eggs and vanilla and beat well with a wooden spoon or with an electric mixer, until all the ingredients are well blended; the mixture should be thick and slightly glossy looking.

2. Drop a good heaped teaspoonful of mixture into each paper cake case, then either put the cases into the sections of a deep patty or muffin tin or stand them on a baking tray. Bake in a preheated oven for 15–20 minutes until the cakes have risen and feel firm to a light touch.
3. Remove them from the oven and leave to cool on a wire rack. When the cakes are cool, spread a little melted chocolate on top of each one.

# DATE AND WALNUT TEA BREAD

MAKES A 450 g (1 lb) LOAF

*175 g (6 oz) cooking dates (not sugar rolled)*
*175 g (6 oz) plain 85% wholewheat flour*
*3 teaspoons baking powder*
*75 g (3 oz) walnuts, chopped*
*½ teaspoon vanilla extract or essence*

**Preparation time:** 15 minutes, plus cooling
**Cooking time:** 50–60 minutes
**Oven:** 180°C, 350°F, Gas Mark 4

**V** Suitable for vegans
1. Grease a 450 g (1 lb) loaf tin and line with greased greaseproof paper. Simmer the dates with 300 ml (½ pint) water until

reduced to a purée. Leave to cool.
2. Sift the flour and baking powder into a bowl. Add the walnuts, vanilla and date mixture. Stir well.
3. Spoon into the prepared tin, and bake in a preheated oven for 50–60 minutes. Cool.

*Variation:* this recipe can also be made with dried apricots.

# BROWN SUGAR FLAPJACKS

MAKES ABOUT 20

*175 g (6 oz) butter or margarine*
*175 g (6 oz) Barbados sugar*
*250 g (9 oz) rolled oats*

**Preparation time:** 10 minutes
**Cooking time:** 20 minutes
**Oven:** 180°C, 350°F, Gas Mark 4

1. Grease an 18 x 28 cm (7 x 11 inch) Swiss roll tin. Put the butter or margarine and sugar into a large saucepan and heat gently until melted, then remove from the heat and stir in the oats. Mix well, then spread the mixture into the tin and press down evenly.
2. Bake in a preheated oven for 20 minutes, until brown all over. Mark into

fingers while still hot, then leave in the tin until cold. The flapjacks become crisp as they cool and will keep well in an airtight tin.

*CLOCKWISE FROM THE TOP: Little brown sugar chocolate buns; Date and walnut tea bread; Brown sugar flapjacks*

# OLD-FASHIONED FRUIT CAKE

MAKES A 20 cm (8 inch) CAKE
*350 g (12 oz) plain 85 or 100 per cent*
*wholewheat flour*
*1 teaspoon ground mixed spice*
*175 g (6 oz) butter or margarine*
*175 g (6 oz) Barbados sugar*
*225 g (8 oz) mixed dried fruit, including*
*candied peel, washed and dried thoroughly*
*on paper towels*
*100 g (4 oz) glacé cherries, rinsed and halved*
*grated rind of 1 well-scrubbed orange*
*25 g (1 oz) ground almonds*
*120 ml (4 fl oz) milk*
*2 tablespoons vinegar*
*¾ teaspoon bicarbonate of soda*

**Preparation time:** 35 minutes
**Cooking time:** 2–2½ hours
**Oven:** 150°C, 300°F, Gas Mark 2

This cake is best fresh, but will keep for 7–10 days if wrapped in greaseproof paper and foil and kept in a tin.
1. Grease a 20 cm (8 inch) cake tin and line with a double layer of greased greaseproof paper. Sift the flour and spice into a bowl, adding the bran from the sieve, too, if you're using 100 per cent wholewheat flour. Rub the fat into the flour with your fingers until the mixture resembles breadcrumbs, then add the sugar, dried fruit, cherries, orange rind and ground almonds.
2. Warm half the milk in a small saucepan and add the vinegar. Dissolve the bicarbonate of soda in the rest of the milk, then add to the milk and vinegar mixture. Quickly stir this into the flour and fruit, mixing well so that everything is combined.
3. Spoon the mixture into the prepared cake tin. Bake in a preheated oven for 2–2½ hours, until a skewer inserted into the centre of the cake comes out clean. Leave the cake in the tin to cool, then strip off the greaseproof paper.

# ALMOND SHORTBREAD

*175 g (6 oz) soft butter or margarine*
*75 g (3 oz) soft brown sugar*
*175 g (6 oz) plain 85 per cent*
*wholewheat flour*
*50 g (2 oz) brown rice flour*
*25 g (1 oz) ground almonds*

**Preparation time:** 20 minutes
**Cooking time:** about 1 hour
**Oven:** 150°C, 300°F, Gas Mark 2

1. Grease an 18 x 28 cm (7 x 11 inch) Swiss roll tin.
2. Cream together the butter and sugar, then beat in the rest of the ingredients. Press the mixture into the tin, prick the top and bake in a preheated oven for about 1 hour or until pale golden.
3. Cool slightly, then cut into fingers.

*One of the most popular nuts in the world, almonds are grown around the Mediterranean and in the Canary Islands and California. They are one of the most useful nuts from the cooks point of view and also one of the richest in iron and protein. Whole blanched almonds are a favourite in cake decorating, while ground almonds add an extra something to cakes, flans, sauces and stuffings. Flaked almonds, toasted or dry-fried, enhance such diverse dishes as salads and ice creams and add the perfect finishing touch to the cream which sandwiches together meringues.*

*FROM THE LEFT: Old-fashioned fruit cake; Almond shortbread*

# ORANGE, ALMOND AND CHOCOLATE CAKE

275 g (10 oz) self-raising 85 per cent
   wholewheat flour
3 teaspoons baking powder
50 g (2 oz) ground almonds
250 g (9 oz) caster sugar
grated rind of 1 orange
9 tablespoons sunflower oil
juice of 1 orange made up to 325 ml (11 fl oz)
   with water

To decorate:
175 g (6 oz) vegan unsalted margarine
175 g (6 oz) icing sugar
2 tablespoons cocoa
little hot water
halved and split blanched almonds
very finely grated orange rind
angelica

**Preparation time:** 30 minutes
**Cooking time:** about 40 minutes
**Oven:** 160°C, 325°F. Gas Mark 3

Suitable for vegans

Although this cake is light and moist, it contains no eggs, and so makes a delicious treat for vegans.
1. Grease and base-line two 20 cm (8 inch) sandwich tins. Sift the flour and baking powder into a bowl. Add the ground almonds, sugar and orange rind. Make a well in the centre and add the oil, then gradually add the orange juice and water mixture, stirring well with a wooden spoon to make a smooth batter.
2. Pour the batter into the tins. Bake in a preheated oven for 40 minutes, or until the

cakes spring back when touched lightly in the centre. Remove from the oven, allow the cakes to cool slightly in the tins, then turn them out on to a wire cooling rack and strip off the greaseproof paper.
3. To make the buttercream, put the margarine, icing sugar and cocoa into a bowl and cream together until light and fluffy. When the cake halves are completely cold, sandwich them together with half the buttercream and spread the remainder on top. Decorate with one or more 'daisies' made from blanched almonds, arranged like petals, with very finely grated orange rind to make the centres, and stems and leaves of angelica.

# CARROT CAKE

100 g (4 oz) plain flour
100 g (4 oz) plain 85% wholewheat flour
2 teaspoons baking powder
150 g (5 oz) soft brown sugar
150 ml (¼ pint) sunflower oil
2 eggs
225 g (8 oz) can pineapple rings, drained and
   chopped
150 g (5 oz) coarsely grated carrot
100 g (4 oz) sultanas
25 g (1 oz) chopped walnuts
25 g (1 oz) walnut pieces, to decorate

Curd cheese frosting:
225 g (8 oz) curd cheese
50 g (2 oz) soft butter or vegetable margarine
50 g (2 oz) soft light brown sugar
½ teaspoon vanilla extract

*FROM THE TOP: Orange, almond and chocolate cake; Carrot cake*

**Preparation time:** 30 minutes, plus cooling
**Cooking time:** 2–2¼ hours
**Oven:** 160°C, 325°F, Gas Mark 3; then: 150°C, 300°F, Gas Mark 2

1. Grease and line an 18 cm (7 inch) round cake tin. Sift the flours and baking powder into a bowl, adding the residue of bran from the sieve as well. Add the rest of the ingredients to the bowl and mix, beating well.
2. Turn the mixture into the cake tin. Bake in preheated oven for 1 hour, then turn the heat down and bake for a further 1–1¼ hours, or until a skewer inserted in the centre comes out clean.
3. Cool in the tin for 30 minutes, then turn out of the tin, strip off the paper and finish cooling on a wire rack. When the cake is completely cold, split it across in half.
4. To make the curd cheese frosting, put all the ingredients into a bowl and beat

thoroughly until smooth. Sandwich the two halves together using half the frosting. Spread the remaining frosting on top of the cake and decorate with walnut pieces.

# SPECIALLY FOR CHILDREN

**O**nce children are past the weaning stage there is no reason why they should not share meals with the rest of the family. However, there are often times when they need to eat earlier, or occasions when the family doesn't eat together. So in this chapter I've gathered recipes for the kind of food which children like, and which is healthy and fairly quick and easy to prepare.

*Fresh Orange Jelly (recipe, page 118)*

## EGG BITES

SERVES 10
*6 slices wholewheat bread from a sliced loaf*
*butter or margarine*

Filling:
*3 hard-boiled eggs, finely chopped*
*2 tablespoons double or whipping cream*
*salt*
*freshly ground black pepper*

**Preparation time:** 20 minutes

Beat a little mayonnaise into the egg as a pleasant alternative to cream.
1. First make the filling. Mix the chopped hard-boiled eggs with the cream and seasoning, mashing them so that the mixture holds together.
2. Spread the bread thinly with butter or margarine, then spread half the slices with the egg mixture.

3. Place the remaining slices of bread on top to make sandwiches, press down firmly, then cut off the crusts. Cut the sandwiches diagonally twice, making each one into 4 triangles.
4. Put the sandwiches on a plate; cover with clingfilm and refrigerate until required.

## FUNNY FACE OPEN SANDWICHES

SERVES 1
*1–2 slices wholewheat bread*
*sesame seed spread or peanut butter*
*1 small carrot, grated, or some cress*
*small piece of tomato*
*2 raisins*
*few sunflower seeds*
*small piece of date*
*triangles of cucumber, carrot or cooked*
    *beetroot*

**Preparation time:** about 10 minutes

ᕓ Suitable for vegans
These are great fun to make and a marvellous way of tempting reluctant eaters! If you do the basic preparation of the bread and ingredients, the children might like to decorate the faces themselves.
1. Using a sharp knife, trim off the corners of the bread to make a roughly circular shape. Spread the bread all over with the sesame seed spread or peanut butter.

2. Press grated carrot or cress around the top edges for hair; position the raisins for eyes, sunflower seeds for eyebrows, a slice of date for the nose and a thin piece of tomato for the mouth. Arrange two triangles of cucumber, carrot or cooked beetroot for a bow tie.

## CHEESE DIPPERS

SERVES 1
*1 teaspoon butter or margarine*
*50 g (2 oz) finely grated cheese*
*2 tablespoons milk*
*2 small carrots, cut into matchsticks*
*2 small celery sticks, cut into matchsticks*
*few sprigs of raw broccoli or cauliflower*

**Preparation time:** 10 minutes

1. Put the butter or margarine into a small bowl and beat until soft, then gradually beat in the cheese and milk to form a soft consistency.
2. Spoon this cheese dip into a small container and stand it in the centre of a larger plate with the prepared vegetables round it.

*FROM THE TOP: Egg bites; Funny face open sandwiches; Cheese dippers*

# YOGURT KNICKERBOCKER GLORY

250 g (9 oz) carton thick Greek yogurt
300 ml (½ pint) raspberry yogurt, preferably
    made with real fruit and sweetened with
    Barbados sugar
2 large bananas, peeled and sliced
50 g (2 oz) hazelnuts, chopped

**Preparation time:** 10 minutes, plus chilling

1. Layer the Greek yogurt, raspberry yogurt and banana attractively in four deep glasses, putting some of the banana slices down the sides of the glasses. Sprinkle the chopped nuts on top.
2. Chill until ready to serve.

# GINGERBREAD MEN

MAKES 6–8
25 g (1 oz) butter
40 g (1½ oz) Barbados sugar
1 tablespoon black treacle
2 tablespoons golden syrup
100 g (4 oz) fine 100 per cent wholewheat
    flour
½ teaspoon bicarbonate of soda
½ teaspoon ground ginger

To decorate:
100 g (4 oz) icing sugar
1–2 tablespoons water
red, green, yellow and blue food colourings

**Preparation time:** 10 minutes, plus cooling
**Cooking time:** 20 minutes
**Oven:** 180°C, 350°F, Gas Mark 4

1. Grease a large baking tray. Put the butter, sugar, treacle and golden syrup into a small saucepan and heat gently until melted. Remove from the heat and allow to cool to tepid.
2. Sift the flour into a bowl with the bicarbonate of soda and ground ginger, adding the bran left behind in the sieve too. Add the melted ingredients to the flour mixture and stir to make a pliable dough.
3. Roll out the dough to about 5 mm (¼ inch) thick and cut into gingerbread men shapes. Bake for about 10 minutes. Cool.
4. To finish the gingerbread men, mix the icing sugar with the water to make a pouring consistency. Divide into 4 and colour each batch with a different food colouring. Make piping bags with grease-proof paper and pipe decorations on the gingerbread men.

# CRUNCHY CAROB BISCUITS

MAKES 24
125 g (5 oz) self-raising 85 per cent
    wholewheat flour
2 tablespoons carob powder
100 g (4 oz) butter or margarine
50 g (2 oz) Barbados sugar
1 tablespoon milk (optional)

**Preparation time:** 10 minutes
**Cooking time:** 10 minutes
**Oven:** 190°C, 375°F, Gas Mark 5

Children love these light, crunchy biscuits.
1. Grease a baking sheet. Sift the flour and carob powder. Cream the butter or margarine and sugar until light, then add the flour mixture. Mix to a dough, adding a little milk, if necessary, to make a firm consistency.
2. Form into 24 small balls, flatten and place on a baking sheet. Bake for 10 minutes. Cool on a wire rack.

*FROM THE LEFT: Crunchy carob biscuits; Yogurt knickerbocker glory; Gingerbread men*

# STRAWBERRY MILK SHAKE

**SERVES 1**

*1–2 tablespoons strawberry yogurt made
with live yogurt, real fruit and Barbados
sugar*
*small glass of milk*

This frothy pink drink is popular, especially
if it's served with one of those extra-wide
drinking straws.
1. Put the yogurt and milk into a blender
or food processor and blend until smooth
and frothy, or whisk well. Pour into a
glass.

# FRUIT SQUARES

**SERVES 2**

*350 g (12 oz) mixed dried fruit, e.g. dates,
raisins, sultanas, dried pears*
*100 g (4 oz) nuts, any type, or a mixture, e.g.
cashews, almonds, walnuts or hazelnuts*
*100 g (4 oz) unsweetened desiccated coconut*
*grated rind of 1 well-scrubbed orange*
*hot water, to blend*
*extra desiccated coconut for coating tin*

**Preparation time:** 15 minutes, plus
setting

**V** Suitable for vegans
1. Put the dried fruit and nuts into a
blender or food processor and process
until finely chopped, then add the coconut
and grated orange rind, and process again,
adding enough hot water to make a firm
paste.

2. Sprinkle a little desiccated coconut into
a 20 cm (8 inch) square tin, press the
mixture on top, then sprinkle with more
coconut and press down well. Put a weight
on top and place in the fridge to firm up.
3. Slice into 2.5 cm (1 inch) squares. These
squares can be eaten as they are or with a
little cream.

# FRESH ORANGE JELLY

**SERVES 1**

*65 ml (2½ fl oz) orange juice*
*¼ teaspoon vegetarian gelatine*
*1 small orange, skin and pith removed, flesh
chopped*

To decorate:
*orange segments*
*sprig of mint*

**Preparation time:** 10 minutes
**Cooking time:** about 6 minutes

**V** Suitable for vegans
1. Put the orange juice into a small bowl
and sprinkle the gelatine over. Leave until
it goes spongy.
2. Put the diced orange flesh into a small
serving dish, pour over the orange juice
mixture and cool. Chill until set. Turn out
and decorate with the orange segments
and a sprig of mint.

*Variation:* other fruits and fruit juices can
be used instead of orange. Try a mixture
of pineapple juice and cubed eating apple.

*CLOCKWISE FROM THE TOP LEFT: Fruit
squares; Strawberry milk shake; Fresh orange jelly*

## CLOWN CAKE

MAKES ONE 23 cm (9 inch) CAKE
*225 g (8 oz) butter or margarine*
*225 g (8 oz) soft brown sugar*
*4 eggs, beaten*
*225 g (8 oz) self-raising 85 per cent
    wholewheat flour*
*4 heaped tablespoons raspberry jam
    (preferably reduced sugar)*

Icing and decoration:
*225 g (8 oz) icing sugar*
*3–4 tablespoons water*
*chocolate sticks*
*1 packet of jelly diamond cake decorations*
*1 glacé cherry*
*silver balls*

**Preparation time:** 20 minutes
**Cooking time:** 20–25 minutes
**Oven:** 180°C, 350°F, Gas Mark 4

This is an easy cake to decorate and looks most effective.
1. Grease and base-line two deep 23 cm (9 inch) sandwich tins. Cream the butter and sugar until very light, pale and fluffy, then gradually add the beaten egg, beating well between each addition. Sift the flour into the mixture and fold it in with a metal spoon.
2. Divide the mixture between the two tins and level the tops. Bake for 20–25 minutes, until the cakes spring back if touched lightly in the centre.

3. Cool on a wire rack. Spread one of the cakes with jam and place the other on top.
4. To decorate the cake, mix the icing sugar with the water to make a pouring consistency; pour over the top of the cake, spreading gently to the edges if necessary.
5. Arrange chocolate sticks and yellow jelly diamonds around the top edge of the cake for hair, jelly diamonds for eyes, eyebrows and mouth and the glacé cherry for a nose. Complete the clown effect by placing silver balls on the clowns cheeks.

## DREAMY ICE CREAM

SERVES 10
*½ vanilla pod, crushed in a mortar with a
    pestle*
*600 ml (1 pint) whipping cream*
*1 x 400 g (14 oz) can condensed skimmed
    milk*
*green or red glacé cherries, to decorate*

**Preparation time:** 10 minutes, plus freezing

This is a very simple ice cream with a deliciously creamy texture.
1. Put the crushed vanilla pod into a bowl with the cream and whip the cream until thick. Add the condensed milk and whip again. Remove the vanilla pod.
2. Pour the mixture into a polythene container and freeze until firm.
3. This ice cream is delicious on its own topped with a decoration of glacé cherries, or with any fresh, ripe or lightly stewed fruit. Alternatively, it can be topped with a sauce made by melting a carob bar with a little milk.

*Using a crushed vanilla pod gives this ice cream a true vanilla flavour. These long black dried pods – they are the seed pod of a climbing orchid native to the forests of tropical America – are expensive but worth buying for their wonderful taste. They can be used several times provided they are washed and thoroughly dried each time. Another way of getting a vanilla flavour for sweet dishes is to keep one or two vanilla pods in a jar of caster sugar. Keep the jar permanently topped up and the vanilla pods will perfume it for a long time.*

*FROM THE LEFT: Clown cake; Dreamy ice cream*

# LITTLE HONEY EGG CUSTARD

**SERVES 1**

*1 egg yolk*
*1 teaspoon clear honey*
*3 tablespoons single cream or milk*
*1 drop of vanilla extract (or essence)*
*little grated nutmeg (optional)*

**Preparation time:** 10 minutes
**Cooking time:** 15–20 minutes

1. This can be quickly and easily cooked in a steamer or in a metal colander or sieve set over a saucepan of simmering water. Half-fill the saucepan with water and heat.
2. Meanwhile, put the egg yolk and honey into a small heat-proof ramekin or small dish and mix together, then add the cream or milk and vanilla and mix again until well blended. Grate a little nutmeg on top if liked, but not for a child under 2 years.
3. Cover the ramekin with a piece of foil then put it in the steamer, sieve or colander, cover with a lid and steam for 15–20 minutes, until the custard is set in the centre.
4. Cool slightly before serving, or chill the custard, which will make it firmer and creamier-tasting.

# FROZEN BANANAS

**SERVES 1**

*1 banana, peeled*
*3 or 4 lolly sticks (optional)*
*1 tablespoon clear honey*
*1 tablespoon chopped almonds or walnuts*
*1 tablespoon carob powder*

**Preparation time:** 30 minutes, plus freezing

Not suitable for children under 5
1. Cut the banana into 3 or 4 pieces and push a lolly stick into each, or slice the banana fairly thickly for a frozen dessert.
2. Put the honey, nuts and carob on to separate plates.
3. Coat the banana pieces thoroughly, first in the honey, then in the nuts, and finally in the carob powder.
4. If you're making ice lollies, place them on a piece of foil; for a frozen dessert, spoon the coated banana pieces into a small freezer-proof bowl.
5. Freeze for about 1 hour, until solid. If the bananas become very hard, allow them to stand at room temperature for 15 minutes or so before serving. Do not serve to children under 5 years old.

# BABY MERINGUES

**MAKES 20 PAIRS**

*flour for sprinkling*
*2 egg whites*
*pinch of cream of tartar*
*100 g (4 oz) Demerara sugar*

Filling:
*300 ml (½ pint) whipping cream*
*pinch sugar*

**Preparation time:** 30 minutes
**Cooking time:** 1½–2 hours
**Oven:** 150°C, 300°F, Gas Mark 2;
then: 110°C, 225°F, Gas Mark ¼

1. Line a baking tray with a piece of greased greaseproof paper, and sprinkle with flour.
2. Put the egg whites into a clean, grease-free bowl with the cream of tartar and whisk until stiff and dry. You should be able to turn the bowl upside down without spilling the egg white.
3. Whisk in half the sugar, then add the remaining sugar and whisk well.
4. Pipe 40 small mounds or drop heaped teaspoonfuls of the mixture on to the prepared baking sheet. Place in the lowest part of the preheated oven, then reduce the setting. Bake for 1½–2 hours, until the meringues are dried out.
5. Turn off the heat and leave the meringues to cool in the oven. Remove them from the tray with a palette knife.
6. Whip the cream and sugar and use to sandwich the meringues in pairs. They can be filled about 1 hour before serving.

*CLOCKWISE FROM TOP LEFT: Frozen bananas; Little honey egg custard; Baby meringues*

# MENU PLANNER

## LUNCH BOXES

Easy tomato soup: page 18

Wheat-filled pittas: page 28

Carrot, banana and pecan salad: page 76

Brown sugar flapjacks: page 107

## BRUNCH

Wild mushroom feuilleté: page 54

Mango compote: page 13

Wheatgerm, honey and raisin muffins: page 13

Oatcakes: page 104

## QUICK SUPPER

Avocado cream: page 53

Stir-fried vegetables with nutballs: page 22

Melba peaches: page 92

## SUMMER DINNER PARTY

Chilled two-colour melon soup: page 42

Spinach roulade with mushroom and soured cream filling: 64

Chunky salad: page 71

Blackcurrant ripple: page 90

## WINTER DINNER PARTY

Watercress and Stilton soup: page 42

Chestnut, walnut and red wine loaf: page 58

Buttered broccoli: page 54

Peach and ratafia trifle: page 88

## CHILDREN'S HIGH TEA

Cheese dippers: page 115

Quick and easy bread, spread with yeast extract: page 100

Fresh orange jelly: page 118

Wholewheat jam tarts: page 104

# $\mathcal{F}$OOD FACTS

## HELEN DORE

# THE VEGETARIAN DIET

A vegetarian diet excludes meat, poultry and fish, and any products such as beef suet, lard and gelatine, which result from the slaughter of animals. Natural dairy products such as milk, cream, cheese and butter do feature in a vegetarian diet, and many vegetarians also eat non-battery, free-range eggs.

There are many reasons for vegetarianism. One is religion – Hindus and Buddhists, for instance, are strict vegetarians. Another is simply the feeling that the raising and killing of animals for food is abhorrent, and this may include the view that, despite the growing interest in humane animal husbandry, the conditions in which animals are bred and slaughtered may all too often cause unnecessary suffering. And in recent years, more and more people are turning to vegetarianism on health grounds. As we

are increasingly advised to cut right down on fat, salt and sugar, and to build up our fibre intake, the vegetarian diet seems especially attractive, offering natural opportunities to follow health advice and improve eating habits, with its emphasis on low-fat, high-fibre pulses, grains and fresh vegetables, on herbs and spices as preferred seasonings to salt, and fresh and dried fruits as natural sweeteners.

As more and more people have become interested in, experimented with, and finally converted to the vegetarian diet for whatever reason, vegetarianism has fortunately now totally lost the rather 'cranky', eccentric image it once had, and has now become very much part of the modern life-style. All the ingredients required for vegetarian cooking at home (pages 128–136) are now to be found in any good supermarket, where you will also

find an increasing range of interesting ready-made vegetarian dishes, ideal for when you are too busy to cook. Many restaurants, too, from top hotels to fast food takeaways, feature vegetarian dishes on their menus, or may even offer a complete alternative vegetarian menu. Exclusively vegetarian restaurants, now found in increasing numbers all over the country, offer excellent opportunities to sample some more unusual vegetarian dishes, and discover for yourself the versatility of the vegetarian diet, which the recipes in this book illustrate so well.

# THE VEGAN DIET

Vegans take the vegetarian diet one step further and exclude from it all animal products including dairy produce, often basing this on the association of the industrial production of milk, eggs, etc. with the undesirable practices of factory farming. In the vegan diet there is strong emphasis on nuts, pulses, grains, fruit and vegetables. Some vegans eat honey; some do not. Dairy milk is replaced by soya milk, high in protein, low in fat and rich in vitamins and minerals. Soya milk is available unsweetened, sweetened and in concentrated form – concentrated soya milk can be used like pouring cream and also to make vegan ice cream and yogurt. Another soya product, tofu, or bean curd, features prominently in the vegan diet: the bland flavour of tofu makes it suitable for

use in a wide variety of sweet and savoury dishes. Smoked tofu has also recently become more widely available. Tofu comes in various textures: the soft type, sometimes called silky tofu, is best for blending; hard-pressed tofu, with its firmer texture, is good for slicing and cubing.

Soft polyunsaturated margarine based exclusively on vegetable oils replaces butter in the vegan diet – kosher margarine, available from Jewish delicatessens, is also vegan. Although eggs are not permitted, vegans can still make very good cakes, using yeast and baking powder as the principal raising agents. Many vegetarian recipes can be adapted for vegan use making these simple substitutions.

## VEGETARIAN PLUS POINTS

Here are just some of the many advantages of the vegetarian diet:

**Natural:** the use of wholefood ingredients like wholemeal flour, unrefined brown rice, wholewheat pasta, natural raw sugar and honey, nature's own sweetener, as well as lots of dried and fresh vegetables and fruit, means that the vegetarian diet is literally the most natural diet.

**Accessible:** the ingredients of the vegetarian diet are now no longer only to be found in obscure specialist health food shops but are now becoming more and more readily accessible on supermarket shelves, making the vegetarian cuisine available to everyone.

**Creative:** vegetarian cooking techniques can be as varied as you like: dips and canapés; soups and sauces; pasta, pancakes and salads; main-course stir-fries, casseroles and nut roasts; desserts and all kinds of baking – the vegetarian cook's repertoire is one to be proud of.

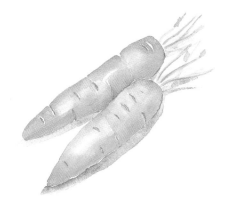

**Variety:** long gone are the days when a vegetarian meal invariably meant a nut cutlet (though this can be delicious!). With so many fresh ingredients to choose from to get the balance of the diet right (pages 128–136) there's no chance of the vegetarian diet ever becoming boring. It's also an inspiration to the cook: the pleasure of cooking with fresh, natural ingredients cannot be over-estimated. Every meal, from a healthy breakfast to a smart dinner party, and from a weekday lunchbox and a children's party to a full Christmas dinner, is delicious the vegetarian way.

**Healthy:** a well-balanced vegetarian diet is undoubtedly very good for everyone and can do much to counter obesity, heart disease, high blood pressure and bowel problems.

**Quick:** crunchy vegetables, leafy salads, fresh and dried fruit dishes, and vegetable and fruit juices mean that snacks and whole meals need involve no cooking at all, making the vegetarian diet ideal for busy people. The microwave does wonders with many vegetarian dishes: jacket potatoes; perfectly cooked mixed vegetables, full of colour, texture and healthy vitamins and minerals; creamy or chunky vegetable soups; poached fruit.

**Economical:** on the whole, vegetarian ingredients cost considerably less than expensive meat and fish, and with a little strategic bulk-buying of items like pulses and grains, shopping around in markets for the freshest fruit and vegetables, and making clever use of your freezer, you'll find that cooking vegetarian does wonders for your budget.

**Stylish:** vegetarian cuisine has completely shed the rather homespun image it once had. A vegetarian dinner or buffet party can be a truly sophisticated affair – see the menu ideas on page 124.

## INCREASING YOUR IRON

It is especially important for vegetarians and vegans to watch their iron intake: iron deficiency is a cause of anaemia.

- Make use of wholewheat pasta for main dishes and serving accompaniments.
- Concentrate on pulses which are highest in iron, such as lentils.
- Eat plenty of dried fruit, especially prunes, in a compote, mixed with breakfast muesli, or as nibbles.
- Bananas have a high iron content, so keep your fruit bowl well stocked with them.
- Raw spinach is rich in iron, so use tender young spinach leaves in salads.
- Watercress is a valuable source of iron, so include it in your salads too.
- Bake potatoes in their jackets to retain maximum iron.
- Use iron-rich wheatgerm to sprinkle on breakfast cereal; add to stuffing and coating mixtures, and use in baking, mixed with flour.

# FRESH VEGETABLES

Vegetable variety lends interest to all kinds of vegetarian dishes – starters, snacks, main courses and accompaniments. The wide range of vitamins and minerals they offer make them one of the most valued ingredients in the vegetarian diet.

## ROOT VEGETABLES AND TUBERS

**Potatoes** really come into their own in vegetarian cuisine. They are full of body-building protein, iron and carbohydrate for energy and can be cooked in so many ways. Floury potatoes baked in their jackets with a savoury topping (see below) make a complete light meal, ideal for lunch or a child's supper. Mashed to a cream, potatoes are a delicious accompaniment, to a vegetarian casserole (page 38) or Nutburgers (page 26); mashed potato may also be piped into attractive swirls and baked, for duchesse potatoes, or shaped, crumbed and fried for croquettes. Roast potatoes would go well with the Chestnut, walnut and red wine loaf (page 58). Scoring them with a fork before roasting makes for extra crispness. Waxy potatoes keep their shape well so are excellent for chips, sliced as a topping for vegetarian hot pots, and in Gratin Dauphinois, and for salads. Tiny new potatoes are perfect cooked in their skins and tossed in melted butter with plenty of chopped mint. Use the skins whenever possible because of their nutritional value.

**Carrots** are a particularly valuable source of vitamin A, essential for the proper functioning of the eyes and mucous membranes throughout the body. New baby carrots are best steamed or microwaved whole; older carrots make good soup (delicious with coriander, as on page 45, or with a dash of orange) and purées, either alone or combined with other root vegetables. Grated raw carrot is good in salads and sandwich and pitta bread fillings; strips of raw carrot are handy, healthy dunks for dips.

**Swede:** often neglected, swede is very good mashed with butter or margarine, then topped with a crumb and cheese mixture for a gratin.

**Parsnips:** these lend a distinctive flavour to soufflés and roulades or soup, and may be roasted like potatoes.

**Turnips:** tiny baby turnips are a real delicacy, delicious glazed or served with a piquant mustard sauce.

**Jerusalem artichokes:** it's well worth the fiddly job of peeling these knobbly tubers, to make wonderfully flavoured creamy soup or crisp, golden fritters.

**Beetroot:** boiled, then skinned and sliced, this is very good with an orange sauce as an accompaniment, or combined with potato and apple in a horseradish dressing for an unusual salad. Beetroot gives rich colour and flavour to vegetarian borsch. Peeled and grated raw beetroot makes a healthy and delicious addition to salads.

## BRASSICAS

**Cabbage** is an excellent source of calcium, essential to the healthy building of bones and teeth. Cabbage is available in different varieties through the year, from crinkly spring Savoy cabbages to firm white or red winter cabbage. Stuffed cabbage leaves make a substantial vegetarian main course dish, baked in a tomato sauce. As an accompaniment, cabbage is best steamed rather than boiled, to avoid wateriness, or stir-fried for an extra-crunchy texture. Firm white or red cabbage shreds well for coleslaw.

**Brussels sprouts:** tender young sprouts are delicious steamed and served with whole chestnuts. They are also good finely shredded in salads. Older sprouts make a smooth purée, to serve as an accompaniment or as the base for a timbale.

**Cauliflower** can be slightly bland and benefits from the addition of a well-flavoured cheese or tomato sauce. It is also excellent curried, in salads, and makes a delicious cream soup.

**Broccoli** is a first-class source of vitamins and minerals, including calcium. Best steamed or stir-fried as an accompaniment, enhanced with melted butter, lemon juice and a few toasted almonds. It also makes a very tasty soufflé. Broccoli stalks, more tender than those of cauliflower, should be sliced and cooked with the florets.

## PODS, STALKS AND SHOOTS

**Peas** are a good source of Vitamin B1, which is needed to ensure a good appetite and general well-being. Peas have a natural affinity with mint; they are also delicious cooked in a little stock with butter and tiny onions.

**Mangetout or sugar peas** are eaten for the pod and are particularly good in stir-fries.

## VEGETARIAN JACKET POTATO TOPPINGS

- grated Cheddar, Edam or Red Leicester
- blue cheese and Greek yogurt
- cottage cheese with chives
- hummus (chick pea and tahina cream)
- pesto (basil and cheese sauce)
- baked beans
- sweetcorn with grated carrot
- mushrooms in soured cream

**Broad beans** are delicious in a creamy herb sauce, and in salads. They also make a very good vegetarian pâté.

**Runner beans:** a favourite summer vegetable accompaniment; when in glut they can be made into a very good chutney.

**French beans** need only topping and tailing to be served as an accompaniment, or mix them with artichoke hearts, olives, tomatoes, hard-boiled eggs and potatoes and toss in a garlicky dressing for a vegetarian version of Salade Niçoise.

**Fennel** has a distinctive aniseed flavour. It is good in soups and soufflés, baked in cheese sauce or sliced raw for salads.

**Celery:** cut into lengths and stuff with cream or blue cheese and nuts for vegetarian canapés. Celery combines beautifully with Stilton in soup as well as for the cheese course. Celery is delicious braised in stock, or chopped raw and combined with apple, raisins, nuts, grated carrot, etc. for winter salads.

**Sweetcorn:** delicious cooked whole and served with butter as a starter. Sweetcorn makes a fine chowder, and is good made into fritters, and in salads and vegetable mixtures.

**Globe artichoke:** a perfect vegetarian starter, boiled and served with a vinaigrette dressing for dipping the base of the leaves, or stuffed. Canned artichoke hearts are excellent storecupboard standbys, for use in salads or as toppings for vegetarian pizza.

**Asparagus:** a good source of folic acid, an important element in cell-formation. Asparagus is the most luxurious of vegetables, wonderful with melted butter or hollandaise sauce, or in soup, as a first course, or to make a vegetarian main course quiche.

**Okra**, also known as ladies' fingers, is popular in African and Caribbean cooking, in curries and stews. A good source of Vitamin A.

MUSHROOMS

A useful source of nutrients, including nicotinic acid, needed for the release of energy from food and the absorption of iron, mushrooms are available in increasing variety in the shops. In the vegetarian diet they are particularly valuable for flavouring purposes and as an ingredient in their own right, for all sorts of substantial main dishes like omelettes, quiches, pizza, bakes. Try mushrooms instead of sausages to make a delicious vegetarian version of toad in the hole. Mushroom starters include Garlic mushrooms (page 58), Mushroom and sherry pâté (page 45) and *à la grecque* (page 62). Dried Italian mushrooms called *porcini* are expensive but make a very useful storecupboard standby for adding intense flavour to stews and sauces.

## PREPARING GLOBE ARTICHOKES

1. Wash and drain the artichoke, cut off the stem and remove any course outer leaves

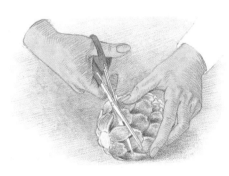

2. Using a pair of kitchen scissors, trim the tops of the lower leaves

3. Cut off the top one third of the artichoke with a sharp knife

4. Using a teaspoon, scoop out the hairy 'choke' and the fibres

## FRUIT VEGETABLES

**Tomatoes** are a prime source of vitamin C, needed for resistance to infection, tissue repair and normal growth. A most versatile vegetable which can be used to make hot or chilled soups; sauces to serve with other vegetables, mousses, roulades and pasta; salads and savoury flans. Large beefsteak tomatoes are ideal for stuffing; tiny cherry tomatoes make pretty garnishes and cocktail nibbles, filled with hummus, cream cheese, etc.

**Peppers:** colourful red, green and yellow sweet peppers are delicious stuffed with savoury mixtures of nuts, grated cheese, rice and other grains, pulses, etc. Peppers may be grilled in vegetable kebabs (page 53), puréed as a filling for pancakes (page 56) or a sauce that is specially good with egg dishes, or sliced and served raw in salads. Chilli peppers with their fiery taste are widely used in curried dishes.

**Avocado:** an almost perfect food, offering a very good balance of protein, vitamins and minerals. Delicious with vinaigrette as a starter; puréed for mousses, dips (page 53) and sandwich spreads; sliced or chopped in a starter (page 72), side or main course salads. Try slices of avocado interleaved with slices of tomato and mozzarella cheese as a satisfying summer main course. Avocados are ideal for stuffing, cold or hot (pages 80 and 64); cooking time for avocados should be brief, or they may become bitter. Lemon juice prevents avocado flesh from discolouring, as will the large stone if buried in an avocado mousse mixture.

## SQUASHES

**Marrow,** served with a rice, pulse or nut filling and served with a fresh tomato sauce is a delicious vegetarian main course. Marrow is also good served as an accompaniment, cubed, steamed and coated in a creamy herb sauce. It also combines very well with ginger in jam.

**Courgettes,** baby marrows, are delicious sliced and steamed, then served with herb butter, or fried in a light batter and sprinkled with lime or lemon juice. Grated courgettes make a pretty green-flecked soufflé or quiche filling.

**Cucumber** is most popular in salads, either mixed with other salad vegetables, or diced or sliced to make a salad in its own right. Cucumber with yogurt and mint makes the refreshing Middle Eastern starter, Tsatsiki (page 20); and a delicious cool summer soup. It is also surprisingly good served hot as an accompanying vegetable.

**Pumpkin:** its rather bland taste is

## CHOPPING ONIONS

1. Pull off the skin, then cut the onion in half through the root

2. Place on a chopping board and slice horizontally

3. Place the cut side of the onion on the board and slice downwards

4. Chop once more to get really tiny pieces

complemented well by warm spices like nutmeg or cinnamon, in a smooth, creamy soup or traditional American pie filling.
**Spaghetti squash:** Cook unpeeled, then scoop out the flesh which will resemble strands of spaghetti and may be eaten like pasta, with a sauce or with melted butter and grated cheese.

## CLEANING LEEKS

*1. Using a sharp knife, trim the top green leaves*

*2. Starting from the top, cut halfway into the leek, from the centre out*

*3. Soak in a bowl, cut end downwards, for about 30 minutes*

*4. Rinse well under running water to remove all remaining dirt*

### BULBS

**Onions:** of the many varieties, Spanish onion has the sweetest, least pungent flavour, and may be stuffed and baked as a main course vegetarian dish. Spring onions are good in salads and stir-fries, and small pickling or button onions make ideal additions to vegetable kebabs (page 53). Red onions are attractive and tasty sliced into rings for salad garnishes.
**Shallot:** use these wherever a mild onion flavour is required, in stuffing mixtures, sauces, salads, etc.
**Leek:** one of the highlights of the vegetarian cuisine, leeks can be cooked in so many ways. Use them for soup (page 18), in vegetable bakes, casseroles and gratins, as a filling for a plate pie, braised in stock, coated with a sauce or puréed as a vegetable accompaniment. Shredded leeks are nice in salads; leeks in vinaigrette with plenty of chopped herbs make an unusual starter. They combine very well with mushrooms.

### LEAFY GREEN VEGETABLES

**Spinach**, a valuable source of iron, is a very versatile vegetable. Tender young leaves need no cooking and are very tasty in salads. Cooked spinach makes good soufflés, gnocchi (page 24) and pasta sauces, as well as traditional Egg Florentine. Spinach roulade with mushroom and soured cream filling (page 64) makes a good dinner party dish.
**Swiss chard** resembles spinach but has thicker white ribs and stalk, which need to be removed before cooking. It is good in stir-fries.

### SALAD LEAVES

Salads feature prominently in vegetarian cuisine, and there is a wide selection of leafy ingredients to lend interest to every salad bowl. Choose from tender round lettuce; crisp and crunchy cos, iceberg and Chinese leaves; oak-leaf lettuce and radicchio for colour. Curly endive with its pleasantly bitter flavour gives a salad a pretty, frilly look; Belgian endive or chicory, with its boat-shaped leaves, makes natural containers for serving children's salads. Smaller salad leaves like cress, watercress and lamb's lettuce give a most attractive finish.

# PULSES

Pulses – dried peas, beans and lentils – are rich in protein, minerals, B vitamins and natural fibre. They are inexpensive, store well and are surprisingly versatile. Use them to make loaves, burgers and bakes; as fillings for vegetables, pancakes and savoury flans, and sauces for pasta; in combination with fresh vegetables in casseroles and curries; cold in salads; blended for pâtés, dips and as fillings for wholemeal rolls and pitta bread.

There is a tremendous variety of different pulses, any of which are available from supermarkets (canned cooked pulses are a very useful storecupboard standby). It is well worth looking in Asian food shops to discover some of the more unusual ones. The following are among the most useful in vegetarian cuisine.

**Adzuki beans:** small, reddish-brown, with nutty, sweetish flavour; particularly good mixed with rice.

**Black-eyed beans:** small and quick-cooking, with attractive kidney shape and creamy colour with distinctive black spot; they make attractive salads and accompaniments.

**Butter beans:** one of the best-known pulses, large and kidney-shaped, with creamy white colour. Very versatile: use in soups, bakes, flans and pies, and creamy-smooth dips.

**Flageolet beans:** small, pale green variety of haricot bean with elegant slender shape;

## COOKING PULSES

- Most pulses require soaking before cooking. Place in a deep bowl or saucepan and cover with their height again in cold water. Leave for 6–8 hours or overnight.
- For a quicker soak, boil for 2 minutes, then leave to soak for 1 hour.
- Drain the soaked pulses, rinse under cold running water, then cover with fresh cold water in a large saucepan, bring to the boil and simmer gently until cooked. Cooking time will depend on the type of pulse and its shelf life. Always buy pulses from a shop with a quick turnover.
- Never add salt to pulses during cooking as this will toughen them. Season after they are cooked.

# GRAINS

Experiment with the many interesting grains in the shops today – rice is just one of them! – and you will not only lend satisfying chewiness to vegetarian dishes;

you will also be adding important sources of iron and fibre to your diet.

**Barley:** wholegrain pot barley is very chewy indeed. 'Pearl' barley, with the husk removed, is easier to digest: a handful added to a vegetable soup or casserole gives good flavour and texture.

**Rice:** brown rice, the whole natural, unprocessed grain, takes longer to cook than polished white rice; cooked by the absorption method it retains maximum food value. For 4 people put 225 g (8 oz) rice and 600 ml (1 pint) cold water into a saucepan with some salt; bring to the boil, then turn the heat down, cover the pan and cook very gently for 40–45 minutes until the rice is tender and all the water is absorbed. Add a knob of butter or margarine and some freshly ground black pepper to the cooked rice. Of white rice,

basmati has the best flavour, and with its long, narrow grains it cooks exceptionally quickly. Italian round-grained is ideal for vegetarian risottos, and short-grain pudding rice is the type to use for creamy desserts.

**Whole wheat:** whole grains from health food shops make good additions to salads. 100% wholemeal flour is milled from the whole wheat grain, with the wheatgerm and bran retained; 85% is lighter, with the coarsest of the bran removed. Use wholemeal flour in all kinds of vegetarian baking: plain for pastry, puddings, rich fruit cakes and gingerbread; 'strong' for bread loaves and rolls; and self-raising wholemeal for lighter cakes, and scones.

**Bulgur wheat or cracked wheat:** cracked and steamed wheat grains are good in stews and salads, especially the Middle

delicious in salads; try mixing with black-eyed beans and butter beans for a Three-bean Salad.

**Red kidney beans:** very tasty and colourful: use to make a robust stew (page 30) or vegetarian chilli (page 28). It is essential to boil these beans hard for 10 minutes at the beginning of cooking, to rid them of harmful toxins.

**Mung beans:** small, round, green, soft-textured; require no pre-soaking before cooking and are good for sprouting (see right).

**Chick peas:** pale in colour, with a wonderful earthy flavour, these are the main ingredient in hummus (page 20), the Middle Eastern dip. Chick peas are also delicious in salads – try them with onion rings, orange segments and watercress, or with cooked spinach and yogurt.

**Split peas:** both yellow and green varieties disintegrate easily and cook down well for soups and purées, and in traditional English pease pudding.

**Lentils:** various types are available. Green and earthy-brown lentils are very good in curries, vegetarian loaves and bakes. Split red lentils are excellent puréed, in dal to accompany vegetarian curry. Green and brown lentils cook in about 45 minutes; red lentils which do not need presoaking, only take 20 minutes.

## SPROUTING BEANS

- Use mung beans, whole lentils or chick peas.
- Place 2 tablespoons of your chosen pulse in a jam jar. Cover with cold water and leave to soak for 8–12 hours.
- Cover with a piece of cheesecloth or muslin and fasten with an elastic band, then drain the water through the cloth.
- Fill the jar with fresh cold water, swish it around and drain again.
- Repeat the rinsing and draining process twice a day for 2–4 days until small shoots have formed.
- Never leave beans soaking in water or they will rot.
- Use the bean sprouts to give crunch to salads, sandwich fillings and stir-fries.

Eastern Cracked wheat salad, sometimes called *tabbouleh* (page 71), a delicious mixture of cracked wheat, lots of chopped parsely and mint, spring onion and fruity olive oil. Bulgar wheat consists of little golden-brown grains which look a bit like Demerara sugar in the packet.

**Couscous,** another pre-cooked grain, is processed from semolina. A north African dish, it is delicious steamed over a bubbling vegetarian casserole, absorbing all the goodness of the vegetables, and then served as an accompaniment.

**Oats:** flaky rolled oats should feature frequently in vegetarian breakfast dishes, like porridge (page 10) and muesli mixtures (page 8). Oatmeal, variously graded into coarse, medium and fine, is good for baking – oatcakes, parkin and flapjacks in particular.

*1. Place the beans in a jam jar*

*2. Cover the jar with a piece of cheesecloth or muslin*

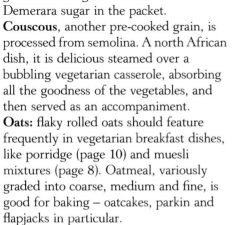

*3. Fill the jar with cold water and rinse and drain twice a day through the cheesecloth*

# FRUIT

Fresh fruit is the most inspring of ingredients for all kinds of compotes, puddings, desserts and cakes, and combined with vegetables in savoury starters or main course salads. Many fruits are valuable sources of fibre, minerals such as iron and potassium, and a variety of vitamins. Always wash fruit very thoroughly and try to eat it unpeeled where possible – so much of the goodness is in the skin.

**Apples:** an excellent source of fibre. Crisp, sweet dessert Cox's Orange Pippin is ideal for apple flans and fritters; red-skinned Starking and green Granny Smith are good in fruit salad (page 95). Bramley's Seedling, Britain's favourite cooking apple, stews down to a light, fluffy purée, ideal for apple sauce, while Howgate Wonder, a newer, less widely available cooker, keeps its shape specially well and so is perfect for pies and crumbles. Dried apple rings and flakes are useful for baking. Apple juice is a useful cooking ingredient as well as good to drink.

**Apricots:** at their very best poached, delicious in a tart, set in a rich custard cream. Dried apricots are particularly good, especially the small Hunza apricots, which contain no preservatives or additives. Use dried apricots for compotes, creams, instant snacks and even to make jam.

**Bananas:** rich in vitamin B6, needed by the body for using and making blood, iron and vitamin C, bananas are an excellent food, very good for children, with whom they are usually very popular. Combine bananas with ice cream and nuts, slice into fruit salads, mash to a cream for chiffon pie filling, or flambé with rum. Banana muesli (page 8) makes a delicious and healthy breakfast. Dried bananas have a very powerful flavour and are good for energy-boosting snacks.

**Blackberries:** this delicious hedgerow fruit gives superb flavour and colour to preserves, pies, crumbles and fools. Blackberry and apple crumbles and pies are particularly delicious.

**Blackcurrants** make excellent jam and jelly and are good for cheesecake toppings, pie fillings, ice creams and sorbet.

**Cherries** are attractive in savoury or fruit salads. They are superb in the French batter pudding of clafoutis, and lend a rich colour and interesting texture to a juicy summer pudding. Both sweet black and sharp red Morello cherries make wonderful jam. Cherry soup is a Scandinavian favourite.

**Cranberries:** you don't have to serve delicious cranberry sauce just with turkey! It makes a perfect accompaniment to a festive vegetarian nut roast too.

**Dates:** large fresh dates are good for stuffing with savoury cheese mixtures, or with Brazil nuts or almond paste for sweet nibbles to serve with coffee. Chopped dried dates make filling steamed puddings, sticky cakes and cookies (page 104).

**Grapefruit:** ideal for a refreshing starter, segmented and combined with melon, avocado, etc., or halved, sprinkled with demerara sugar and sherry and grilled until caramelized. Rosy pink grapefruit segments make pretty additions to fruit salads.

**Grapes:** choose from jet black, russet red, white and tiny green seedless grapes, according to season. A mixture of different coloured grapes arranged in concentric circles looks stunning in a flan or on top of cheesecake.

**Kiwi fruit:** sliced to reveal beautifully patterned jade green flesh, these New Zealand fruit lend a decorative touch to all kinds of cold desserts and savoury and sweet salads.

**Kumquats:** these tiny oval oranges can be eaten unpeeled. They make a delicious preserve and pretty garnishes for salads and drinks.

**Lemons:** very useful as a flavouring ingredient, to add sharpness to stuffing mixtures, marinades, dressings and sauces, as well as a delicious zesty flavour to puddings, cakes and icings. Home-

## LIME TWISTS

1. Slice the lime thinly, then make a cut halfway through the slice

2. Twist the two sides of the slit in opposite ways and fold round

## PREPARING A MANGO

1. Slice through the mango on each side as close to the stone as possible

2. Using a dessert spoon or teaspoon scoop out the flesh

3. Alternatively, turn the sides of mango flesh side out and cut into diamonds or cubes without cutting through the skin

4. Peel the skin from the middle section of the mango and cut the flesh away from the stone

segments are delicious in savoury main course or side salads (page 72). The juice is an extremely popular drink, either by itself or as a mixer. To get the most juice from an orange, place it in a bowl of boiling water for 5 minutes before squeezing.

**Peaches:** delicious in mixed salads, and hot or cold desserts. Peaches may be very

## CUTTING ORANGE SEGMENTS

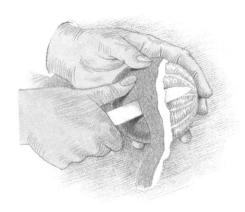

1. Peel the skin from the orange removing all the pith

2. Carefully cut down between each membrane to free the segments

made lemonade is the most refreshing of drinks.

**Limes:** Use like lemons. Lime gives a particularly subtle, fragrant flavour to mousses and cold soufflés, and the attractive green rind and flesh make a nice garnish.

**Mango:** the perfumed flavour and butter-smooth orange flesh make this one of the most delicious exotic fruits. Superb sliced for a perfect breakfast or dessert, or in ice cream, fools and sorbet.

**Melon:** choose from yellow honeydew, greenish ogen, pinkish-orange charentais, and deep pink water melon, to name but a few varieties. Serve chilled as a refreshing starter, or cubed or scooped into balls for fruit salads. Melon also makes delicious sorbet. Water melon shells make an original container for fruit salads.

**Oranges:** valuable sources of vitamins A and C, these are among the healthiest of fruits. Orange gives tangy flavour to many cakes, biscuits and puddings, and the

successfully bottled in brandy. Also available dried. Nectarines are a smooth-skinned variety of peach and can be substituted in most peach recipes.

**Pears:** poached in wine (page 84), baked in tarts and puddings (page 90), or made into stylish sorbet, juicy, succulent pears are a real fruit treat at any time. Choose from Comice and Conference early in the year, Williams later on in the summer. Dried pears are included in dried fruit salad mixtures.

**Pineapple:** a good buy at the beginning of the year, pineapple is good in savoury salads and combines well with lentils in a loaf or bake. Sliced into rings and sprinkled with kirsch it makes an easy yet elegant dessert, and looks good as a buffet centre-piece hollowed out and used as a natural container for an exotic fruit salad.

**Plums:** both dessert and cooking varieties are available. Victoria plums are dual-purpose, making them Britain's favourite plum, for pies, crumbles and jam. Prunes, which are dried plums, make a surprisingly delicious mousse.

**Raspberries:** a delicious soft fruit that is a rich source of fibre. Use in fillings for gâteaux and pavlovas, on cheesecake or in creamy rippled fools and ice creams. Sieved raspberries make a lovely easy sauce.

**Rhubarb:** makes an unusual fruit soup, and is delicious baked with orange or made into a jelly. It makes a juicy pie filling and squashy, squidgy puddings.

**Strawberries:** this favourite summer fruit is also rich in vitamin C. It is not only superb in creamy fools, mousses and pavlovas and shortcakes, it also makes a delicious savoury salad ingredient. Try strawberries sliced with cucumber.

# VEGETARIAN COOKING WITH NUTS

Nuts are concentrated sources of protein, vitamins and minerals, and can be used in various ways to lend substance to vegetarian cuisine.

Vegetarian recipes often require nuts to be grated or ground: this is most easily done in a blender or food processor: blend just until chopped as required, or for ground nuts, process to a powder.

**Soups:** use ground almonds, Brazils or cashews, or chestnut purée, in combination with fresh vegetables to make creamy, warming soups, which can be filling enough to make a light meal in themselves, accompanied by wholemeal bread or rolls.

**Main courses:** hazelnuts, Brazil nuts, cashews, peanuts, walnuts and pine nuts make very good burgers, rissoles, nutballs, bakes and roasts, either individually or combined with other nuts chopped and mixed with wholemeal breadcrumbs, herbs, spices and other flavourings like soy sauce, yeast extract, grated cheese, etc. Chestnuts make a specially festive Christmas roast. Serve with fresh herb, tomato or cranberry sauce.

**Salads:** mix any kind of nut with fresh vegetables and pulses or grains to make substantial main course salads.

**Stuffings:** use chopped nuts in fillings for vegetables like mushrooms, tomatoes, aubergines, marrow.

**Sauces:** ground almonds, walnuts, peanuts or hazelnuts make delicious sauces for dipping fried tofu cubes, vegetable kebabs (page 53), etc. Peanut butter mixed with hot stock to the desired consistency makes a useful instant nut sauce when you are in a hurry.

**Coatings and toppings:** use chopped nuts mixed with breadcrumbs, grated cheese, etc. to coat potato croquettes or as a crisp topping for vegetable gratins. Mix chopped toasted nuts in fruit crumble mixtures, scatter on mousses or press on to the sides of a cold soufflé.

**Cakes and biscuits:** Coconut and walnuts are favourite cake flavourings. Chopped nuts are good in teabreads. Whole Brazils and blanched almonds combined with glacé fruits make splendid cake toppings. Almonds, hazelnuts and peanuts in particular make crisp, crunchy cookies.

**Puddings:** use chopped almonds with honey and rosewater as a filling for layers of phyllo pastry, to make Middle Eastern baklava. Pecan nuts make a superb all-American pie, and pistachios, with their bright green colour, look and taste wonderful in ice-cream.

# THE VEGETARIAN RAW DEAL

The vegetables and fruits which are the staple ingredients of vegetarian cuisine are best eaten raw wherever possible. This way, you get the full benefit of the vitamins and minerals they have to offer.

## SALADS
Salads are one of the most appetizing ways of eating raw vegetables and fruit. There is a whole section of salad recipes on pages 66–81.

Here are a few more suggestions for salads using ingredients that require no cooking at all, some combining vegetables and fruit. Try them with one of the dressings on page 138, a really well-made dressing transforms any salad.

- Sliced radish, bean sprouts and sweetcorn
- Tomato, basil and spring onion
- Shredded Brussels sprouts, grated carrot, chopped dates and orange segments
- Chinese leaves, apple, blue cheese and nuts
- Cottage cheese, strawberry, peach and shredded cos or iceberg lettuce
- Sweet peppers stuffed with curd cheese, sliced in rings and served on a bed of radicchio, lamb's lettuce and cress
- Pineapple, celery and almond

For an all-fruit salad, it's fun to go for a red- or green-only theme. Choose from the following in season:

| **Red Fruit Salad:** | **Green Fruit Salad:** |
| --- | --- |
| Cherries | Green grapes |
| Raspberries | Kiwi fruit |
| Redcurrants | Avocado |
| Strawberries | Green-skinned apple |
| Red grapes | Ogen melon |
| Red-skinned apple | Pear |
| Rosy grapefruit | Grapefruit |

## PICNICS AND LUNCH BOXES
Try and include fresh raw vegetables and fruit in sandwiches, rolls, baps and pitta pockets whenever possible. Here are some filling suggestions:

- Grated carrot and grated Edam cheese
- Sliced cucumber, cream cheese and cress
- Banana, chopped nuts and honey
- Mashed avocado and curd cheese
- Cottage cheese and pineapple
- Hard-boiled egg, mayonnaise and watercress
- Beansprouts and peanut butter
- Vegetable pâté and sliced tomato
- Cheddar cheese and date

A selection of crunchy vegetable sticks, such as celery stalks, carrot matchsticks, strips of sweet pepper and cucumber, is also a good addition to a lunchbox; they can be eaten by themselves or to scoop up a savoury dip packed in a rigid container. Cherry tomatoes can be tucked into a child's lunchbox. Always try to include a piece of fresh fruit as well – bananas, satsumas and small apples are specially easy for children to eat. A mixture of dried fruit and nuts would be good too.

# DRINKS

An exciting range of fresh vegetable and fruit juices is available from good supermarkets and health food shops, in bottles, cans and cartons. It is also easy to make your own juices at home using a special juicer.

It is fun to experiment with combinations of fruit and vegetable juices. Try the following:
Carrot and apple
Tomato, carrot and orange
Blackcurrant and apple
Grape and guava

**Exotic fruit cocktail**
Mix equal quantities of peach nectar and passion fruit and pineapple juice. Top up with ice cubes.

**Citrus cocktail**
Mix equal quantities of orange and grapefruit juice and add fresh lime juice to taste. Decorate with slices of lime.

**Apple cooler**
Mix two-thirds apple juice with one-third sparkling mineral water. Add chopped fresh mint and ice cubes.

**Party cup**
Mix equal quantities of chilled apple juice, orange juice and dry white vermouth. Add orange, apple and cucumber slices, sprigs of fresh mint and ice cubes.

# SALAD DRESSINGS

## VINAIGRETTE

Use to dress leafy salads and mixed vegetable salads: if the vegetables are cooked, toss them in the dressing while they are still hot. The basic dressing may be varied by the addition of crushed garlic, tarragon, basil or chives.

*1 tablespoon Dijon mustard*
*½ teaspoon sugar or honey*
*½ teaspoon salt*
*1 tablespoon wine vinegar*
*4 tablespoons olive oil or sunflower oil*

1. Combine the mustard, sugar and salt in a small bowl and gradually stir in the vinegar.
2. Gradually beat in the oil to make a thick mixture.

## MAYONNAISE

*2 egg yolks*
*¼ teaspoon salt*
*¼ teaspoon mustard powder*
*freshly ground black pepper*
*2 teaspoons wine vinegar*
*2 teaspoons lemon juice*
*200 ml (7 fl oz) olive oil or sunflower oil*

1. Put the egg yolks, salt, mustard, pepper, vinegar and lemon juice into a bowl and whisk well until thoroughly blended.
2. Add the oil, drop by drop, whisking all the time.
3. When half the oil has been added and the mixture is thick, add the oil in a thin, steady stream, whisking vigorously all the time, until thick and creamy.

## CREAMY MUSTARD DRESSING

This dressing is delicious with potato salad.

*1 tablespoon Dijon mustard*
*150 ml (5 fl oz) single cream*
*1–2 teaspoons clear honey*
*salt*
*freshly ground black pepper*
*2 teaspoons chopped mixed herbs*

1. Put the mustard into a small bowl and stir in the cream until smooth.
2. Add the honey, salt and pepper to taste and the herbs. Stir well to mix.

## TOMATO DRESSING

This has a very fresh flavour and is delicious with summer salads. If you like a very smooth dressing, de-seed the tomatoes before using. Omitting the oil gives a very low-calorie dressing, ideal for slimmers.

*2 large tomatoes, skinned and quartered*
*1–2 tablespoons olive oil (optional)*
*½ teaspoon mild paprika*
*3–4 drops Tabasco sauce*
*salt*
*freshly ground black pepper*
*few drops of lemon juice or wine vinegar*

1. Put the tomatoes, oil if using, paprika and Tabasco into a blender and blend until smooth. Season with salt, pepper and lemon juice or vinegar to taste.

# BALANCED EATING

As with any diet, it is important for vegetarians and vegans to achieve the right balance of foods for their daily needs. Meal planning should involve the use of ingredients that will supply all the nutrients required for health, in the right proportions. Follow a simple basic eating plan by including all of the following in your daily diet:

**Calcium-rich foods** for strong bones, skin and teeth, and healthy functioning of the heart: at least 1 serving:
Dairy products like milk, cheese and yogurt; leafy green vegetables (especially broccoli and cabbage), dried figs, sesame seeds

**Other protein foods:** at least 2 servings:
Eggs, pulses, nuts, seeds

**Foods for carbohydrates and fibre,** needed for energy and a healthy digestive system: 2–3 servings:
Wholemeal bread and pastry or cakes; grains such as brown rice, barley, couscous; wholewheat pasta, potatoes

**Fresh fruit and vegetables,** for balanced intake of vitamins and minerals: at least 2 servings
Make sure you eat 1 serving of *raw* fruit or vegetables each day.

# A WEEK'S VEGETARIAN MENUS

| | BREAKFAST | LUNCH | EVENING MEAL |
|---|---|---|---|
| **Sunday** | Banana Muesli (page 8) Wholewheat bread & honey | Carrot and Coriander Soup (page 45) Chestnut, Walnut & Red Wine Loaf (page 58) | Colourful Cabbage Salad (page 80) Cheese and fresh fruit |
| **Monday** | Hunza Apricots with Thick Yogurt (page 10) Almonds | Salad sandwiches Dates and nuts | Couscous with Spiced Vegetable Stew (page 33) Blackberry Fool (page 86) |
| **Tuesday** | Porridge (page 10) with raisins Wholewheat toast | Greek Salad (page 79) Orange or apple | Red Bean Stew with Millet Pilaff (page 30) Fresh fruit |
| **Wednesday** | Grated apple, yogurt & wheatgerm | Wheat-filled pittas (page 28) with salad Nuts and raisins | Flaky Mushroom Roll (page 61) Chicory, Orange and Watercress Salad (page 72) Yogurt Knickerbocker Glory (page 116) |
| **Thursday** | Museli Banana or a few grapes Nuts and raisins | Deep-Dish Salad Bowl (page 68) Piece of fresh fruit | Vegetable Gratin (page 33) Beansprout and Red Pepper Salad (page 74) Fruit salad (page 95) |
| **Friday** | Wholewheat cereal with nuts and raisins Toast | Jacket potato with watercress and tomato | Nutburgers in Soft Baps (page 26) Ratatouille (page 35) Melba Peaches (page 92) |
| **Saturday** | Fresh orange and grapefruit segments Wheatgerm, Honey and Raisin Muffins (page 13) | Vegetable soup with Nori (page 18) Pears | Garlic Mushrooms with French bread (page 58) Spinach Gnocchi (page 24) Green salad Mango Sorbet with Honey and Cardamom Sauce (page 86) |

# INDEX

# ACKNOWLEDGEMENTS

Photography
**SUE ATKINSON**

Photographic styling
**CAROLYN RUSSELL**

Preparation of food for photography
**ANNE HILDYARD**

Illustrations
**CHRIS JONES**

Step-by-step illustrations
**PATRICIA CAPON**

Cover photograph
**VERNON MORGAN**

Preparation of food for cover photography
**ALLYSON BIRCH**

The publishers would also like to thank Elizabeth David Ltd.
of 46 Bourne Street, London, SW1, for lending the plates used
in the photograph on page 45